# MARRIED AND LONELY

*Along the Journey of Kingdom Women*

Copyright © 2025 Jasmine Gordon

All Rights Reserved

No portion of this book may be reproduced, stored in a retrieval system, or transmitted by any means electronic, mechanical, photocopy recording, scanning, or other except brief quotations without the prior written permission of the publisher, except in case of brief quotations embodied in critical reviews and certain other noncommercial uses permitted by copyright law.

Unless otherwise indicated, all Scriptures are taken from the King James Version of The Holy Bible.

Reference:
*The 8 Types of Love According to Ancient Greek: Primarily Attributed to the Writings of the Greek Philosopher Plato.*

Disclaimer: The information provided in this book is not meant to be and should not be taken as counseling or teaching. This book was written solely to encourage, empower, enlighten, and uplift my readers.

For permission requests, write to the author at:
mwb8870@gmail.com

Editor:
Shairon Parks & Scribendi

Interior Layout & Design:
Tarsha L. Campbell

Published by:

www.mwbint.org
Email: mwb8870@gmail.com
718.781.0671 | 804.720.6080

To: _____

From: _____

May the God of Abraham, Isaac, and Jacob be with you and see you through all of your challenging moments. May He remain with you and your family continuously. After reading this book, I pray that there will be an undeniable transformation—spiritually, physically, emotionally and psychologically.

—*Jasmine Gordon*

*"When you choose to forgive, consider the healing power being released in your life. Imagine the relief and freedom that come with experiencing peace of mind, along with personal and spiritual growth."*

# Author's Opening Prayer

Abba Father, in the name of Jesus Christ of Nazareth, I come boldly before your throne of mercy on behalf of the readers. Omniscient Father, you are the all-knowing God. You know if the person holding this book is married, single, divorced or widowed. You see their needs, their struggles, challenges, hurt, pain and everything that perplexes them. In the mighty name of Jesus, I ask you to remove all cloudiness, confusion, and frustration from their minds. Heal their minds, O God, I pray.

Father God, open their minds to understand what you are saying to them through this book. Please give them the wisdom to make application of what they learn through your Word and this book. I lift up the homes that are in turmoil and call for the restoration of peace, a breakthrough in their finances, and sincere love and respect in their marriages.

Mighty God, with the turning of each page, may the readers find answers to their many questions. Thank you, Father, for each reader experiencing total deliverance from the spirits of oppression, depression, and loneliness. In the name of Jesus, I command the restoration of uncontrollable desire for one another in each marriage. Omnipotent Father, you are all powerful. I pray this book eliminates obscurities and gives marriages a new zest for life. Lord, may they walk in their victory and extend praises to you.

In Jesus' mighty name, I pray. Amen.

*"Vision is an internal compass that guides you as you navigate your way toward your destiny. Activate your vision."*

## DEDICATION

It is a pleasure to dedicate this study guide to every woman, especially kingdom women who are burdened by all of their duties and having trouble balancing them. To the women who believe that they will continuously walk on "cloud nine," may this book usher in the balance you need in your life.

To the wives who are at their wit's end and on the brink of giving up: if you're feeling frustrated and living with regret, I dedicate this book to you. With each page, may you identify your purpose, find solutions to fix or enhance your marriage, and maximize your full, God-given potential. May you experience the awesome peace and unique power of a godly marriage.

*"It's time to be unshackled and unburdened so you can embrace the undeniable peace of God, enjoy restful sleep, and experience unexplainable Joy as you await your unfading inheritance."*

# Table of Contents

**Epigraph** . . . . . . . . . . . . . . . . . . . . . . . . . . 12

**Acknowledgments** . . . . . . . . . . . . . . . . . . . . .13

**Foreword** . . . . . . . . . . . . . . . . . . . . . . . . . . 14

**Preface** . . . . . . . . . . . . . . . . . . . . . . . . . . . 16

**Introduction** . . . . . . . . . . . . . . . . . . . . . . . 19

**The Woman** . . . . . . . . . . . . . . . . . . . . . . . 22

- Gliding on Cloud Nine
- The Adorning
- Freedom
- Discernment
- What You Should Know Before and After You Say "I Do"

**The Wife** . . . . . . . . . . . . . . . . . . . . . . . . . . 58

- Being a Pastor's Wife
- Love God's Way
- Do Not Let Your Temper Control You
- Say Goodbye to Ego and Pride
- Help-Meet
- Married and Lonely

**The Marriage** . . . . . . . . . . . . . . . . . . . . . 125

- Ten Misses That Can Cause a Rift or Divorce
- Communication
- Respect His Role as a Husband
- Be an Extraordinary Listener
- Forgive Without Compromising
- Be Best Friends
- Teach Your Husband How to Treat You
- Keep the Fire in the Fireplace—Fan the Flames

# Table of Contents

**The Home** . . . . . . . . . . . . . . . . . . . . . . . . . 217

- Do Not Overlook Your Children
- An Inviting Atmosphere
- Take Off the Heels
- Submission
- It Is a Thin Line
- Balance

**The First Lady** . . . . . . . . . . . . . . . . . . . . . . 273

- Respect His Office as Pastor
- Support His Ministry/Ministries
- The Church Face
- Avoid Cliques
- Protect Your Ear Gate
- Never Take Sides
- Be an Attentive Listener
- Delegate
- Intercede

**The Church** . . . . . . . . . . . . . . . . . . . . . . . . 352

- Teach Your Members How to Treat You
- Do Not Let Your Guard Down
- Express Sincerity to the Members
- Do Not Be Quick to Quit
- Do Not Sweat the Small Stuff
- Choose Your Words Wisely
- Do Not Settle for Mediocrity
- Avoid Church Bullies
- Ministries/Departments

## Table of Contents

**Final Thoughts**..................420

**Closing Prayer**..................424

**Interactive Questions and Tips for Your Spouse**............425

**About the Author**..................430

# Epigraph

"All relationships have one law in common. Never make the one you love feel alone, especially when you are there."
-K Upright

"There are no vacations, days off, sick leave or PTO in marriage."

"If you have salvation on a layaway plan, it is time to pick it up. It is paid for in full."

"The spirit of excellence is in existence when there is no audience."
-Jasmine Gordon

"In the quiet of shared nights, a silent yearning for a love that cannot be found."

"The weight of a wedding ring, a heavy reminder of the distance between two hearts."

"A love story written in ink, but the pages remain blank, filled only with the echoes of unspoken words."
-Authors Unknown

# Acknowledgments

First and foremost, I acknowledge the Holy Spirit for the inspiration to pen this study guide, which I hope will be soul-stirring and eye-opening for my readers.

A special thank you to my sisters, Celes and Joy, who sat with me night after night during my writing process. Without a frown or sign of disgust, you listened while I read you the unedited version of my manuscript. I truly appreciate you both for your love and support.

To my pastor, Marsha Minott, thanks for the tough love and the teaching, coaching, and tutoring. You have shaped me into the woman I am today. May the blessings of the Lord shower upon you.

To Keith Miller of Crown Light Studio, I greatly appreciate your input, words of encouragement, and enlightenment. Thank you for believing in me and my projects. You are an excellent cheerleader.

Last, but not least, to my supporters and church family, I am most grateful for your relentless prayers. Thank you all!

## FOREWORD

*As* women, we often wear various hats throughout life. I believe it must have been encoded in our divine makeup to carry the weight of multiple responsibilities throughout our lifetime. We catch a glimpse of this supercharged, God-initiated capability when God declared He would make a "help meet" for His newly-created man, Adam.

And the LORD God said, It is not good that the man should be alone; I will make him an help meet for him.
Genesis 2:18 KJV

If you study the meaning of "help meet" in the original Hebrew language, you will find it simply means "one who helps." This meaning sheds light on one of our Creator's intents for women. We were equipped and empowered to "help meet" on multiple levels. I strongly believe it's not just married women who have been called and designated to be a help meet to their husbands; but the term "help meet" is an attribute of all women—single and married alike. **Women are simply designed to help meet a goal, help meet a budget, help meet a destination, help meet a standard, and the list could go on and on.** Being a help meet is our M.O.—our modus operandi, which is how something operates or works.

That said, I believe that stepping into any leading lady role of being a wife requires great wisdom and flexibility to navigate this territory. In my experiences of counseling and walking alongside wives, I can undoubtedly say it's not always a cakewalk. Depending on where her husband's term of service places them, the complexity of her duties as a wife, along with the expectations placed on her by others, this role can be a daunting task. I advise any woman desiring and seeking to walk in this coveted role to know what she is signing up for. It's certainly not all

# Foreword

glitz and glamour. Being a wife a wondeful expericence. It can also be a lonely journey filled with misunderstandings and misaligned intentions by others to hurt you. On top of that, you must factor in the other hats a kingdom woman could be wearing to "help meet" the expectations of being a mother, sister, friend, career, or businesswoman. I encourage any kingdom woman stepping into the role of a wife to build a strong support system and seek out empowering resources like this book.

Hats off to Evangelist Jasmine Gordon, who I affectionately call "Jasmine the Great" because of her plethora of God-given gifts and talents. I acknowledge and salute her for the loving care and diligence she has employed to write this helpful guide for kingdom women called to be wives. With calculated precision, godly wisdom and prayerful tact, Evangelist Gordon has composed a poignant exposé on what wives may endure, along with solutions on how to respond to such challenges. Evangelist Gordon has certainly fulfilled her role as "help meet" in helping her fellow sisters who may find themselves wearing this coveted hat as a kingdom woman. You are invited to be empowered and grow by utilizing all she has presented in this insightful resource.

Respectfully,

Tarsha L. Campbell
*Minster, Author, Certified Empowerment Coach*
TarshaCampbellEmpowers.com

# Preface

Kingdom Women are not the only ones plagued by loneliness; it is a human condition that can deprive anyone of genuine friends and companionship.

*Married and Lonely: Along the Journey of Kingdom Women* is like a mirror that shows us the reflection of ourselves in all our forms. Indeed, the journey as a follower of Christ can be very lonely. Perhaps you have noticed that before you became a born-again believer, you had many friends and associates, but when you decided to make a U-turn back to Jesus, they vanished. Some people saw you as weird, a fanatic, and weak-minded. Be prepared, because along your journey, everything that is connected to you may undergo attack from the enemy.

Dr. Myles Munroe once said, "When we die, we should die empty." My interpretation of this statement is that we should give all we can, share all we know, and complete all God-given assignments while we are alive.

I know that God sent me to Earth to transform the lives of those whose paths I cross. Therefore, I can no longer stand by and watch marriages and ministries dissolve, knowing that I have the tools to make a difference.

My existence must have a positive impact. I refuse to allow fear, intimidation, or the opinion of others to prevent me from empowering, encouraging, enlightening, and uplifting my sisters and brothers. No person or multitude should suffer in pain because a "servant" lacks the confidence and boldness to intervene.

I refuse to leave this Earth without delivering the life-transforming messages with which I have been entrusted. It would be tragic to find out later that some people lived in lack, misery, and pain because I

## Preface

withheld information and failed to equip and empower them because of my feelings of fear and inadequacy. For this reason, I chose to dispel my fear, sense of inferiority, and lack of confidence. They were already on life support, and I simply pulled the plug.

Moses believed he was unqualified to speak or lead God's people out of bondage. And Moses said unto the Lord, O my Lord, I am not eloquent, neither heretofore, nor since thou hast spoken unto thy servant: but I am slow of speech, and of a slow tongue (Exodus 4:10).

When the angels called Gideon a "mighty man of valor," and God expressed His desire to use him to bring deliverance and freedom to the oppressed people, Gideon doubted. And he (Gideon) said unto him, Oh my Lord, wherewith shall I save Israel? Behold, my family is poor in Manasseh, and I am the least in my father's house (Judges 6:15). Gideon viewed this challenge from a purely physical standpoint; He believed he could not rise to meet it because no one in his family had ever done anything significant. Therefore, he doubted his ability to carry out such a daunting task.

I can imagine the fear, inferiority, and doubt that gripped Gideon. His doubt was so strong that he tested God three times to be sure that He really chose him for such a mighty exploit (Judges 6:36-40). Countless others in the Bible strongly doubted God's call on their lives to take on a specific task because they felt incapable.

Like those men, I am not exempt from fear, doubt, and feelings of inferiority. Never in my wildest dreams did I ever think I would be assigned to write this book. I am in good company, as I, too, feel unqualified for the assignment. However, I attribute my knowledge in

## Preface

this area to the teaching and revelation of the Holy Spirit. In viewing the lives of kingdom women and listening to their stories, and in my personal experience as a woman, a kingdom woman, and a wife, I have gathered valuable information, which I am grateful to offer to you along your journey.

COVID-19 wreaked havoc on many marriages, ministries, lives, homes, businesses, and so on. Yet, many have testified of their blessings due to the pandemic. I do not know your personal story; however, I hope you found peace, blessings, favor, and a new zest for life amid the pandemic. I hope your marriage and friendship have strengthened and that your love and appreciation for each other have grown tremendously. Most importantly, I pray that your love for God and human souls has skyrocketed.

## INTRODUCTION

# Married and Lonely:
# Along the Journey of Kingdom Women

*But seek ye first the kingdom of God, and his righteousness; and all these things shall be added unto you. (Matthew 6:33)*

*Why am I married and lonely?*

Have you ever asked yourself that question? Are you a *wife who is at her wit's end*? Are you frustrated, regretful, and considering giving up on your marriage?

When a woman decides to give her heart and hand to a man in marriage, she expects companionship, an unbreakable union, pampering, attention, and to live happily ever after. Solitude and desertion are never on her radar. If you, as a kingdom woman, desire change in your life, marriage, or ministry, you have the blueprint for the solution in your hands. This book aims to minister to women who think they are superwomen and can do it all as they attempt to balance home, work, ministry, children, and marriage on a tightrope.

*Married and Lonely: Along the Journey of Kingdom Women* is not only about marriage, but about various aspects of life that you will encounter or engage in along your journey as a kingdom woman. *This guide* will encourage, empower, enlighten, and guide you as you navigate the changes and uncertainties in your home and ministry. It will provide you with ways to cope with difficulties and conquer any giant that stands in your way along the journey. If you are married and lonely, perhaps you have already decided to quit your marriage. Hold on, not so fast! This book will assist you in meeting what may be a seemingly insurmountable challenge and rising victoriously.

I wrote this book to give you a new perspective on marriage, life, ministry, people, and the love of God. By reading and working through the exercises you will be inspired to boldly take the following steps toward healing and wholeness in your marriage and ministry.

Kingdom women recognize their inadequacy and powerlessness in sustaining themselves spiritually and materially. Therefore, with humility, they sincerely seek the kingdom of God before they engage in any endeavor, as encouraged in Scripture (Matthew 6:33). They understand that it is only by completely surrendering their mind, body, and soul and trusting the King to lead and direct their lives daily that they can overcome the enemy's plot.

Kingdom women are viewed by many people as a cut above the rest and are held to a high standard. Because they are considered to be a role model, their lives are intensely scrutinized, as they are expected to exhibit perfection, set an example, and embody the spirit of excellence. However, they will quickly remind you that they are far from perfect and totally depend on God every moment of the day to meet these expectations.

One might assume that women who surrender to the King and His kingdom, exemplify Christ in their actions, strive for righteousness,

## Introduction

and find joy in the Holy Ghost would be exempt from troubles, trials, or woes. Unfortunately, however, kingdom women are not exempt from heartache, disappointment, discouragement, doubt, loneliness, or fear. Whether you are an evangelist, missionary, teacher of the Word, minister, or pastor's wife, you will face many pitfalls and obstacles along your life's journey. Bear in mind, though, that you will not go through those troubled times alone. Jesus, the King of kings, is with you always, as He promised never to leave or forsake you.

After reading this book, you will be empowered to be the best helpmeet to your husband. You will be guided in how to gain his attention through effective communication. You will be enlightened about how to establish a balance between your home and ministry, between your husband and church members, and between your personal and church duties. You will be encouraged to love *God's way* and become a more supportive, godly wife. Last, but certainly not least, this book will instruct you on how to keep the passion and fire burning in your marriage.

After each chapter, there are questionnaires to assist you in identifying the root cause of the issue at hand as you brainstorm with your spouse on how to solve the problems you face in your marriage. In honestly and sincerely answering the questions, you may experience moments of enlightenment and clarity regarding your issues. You will be able to delve deeply into unresolved issues, find answers, and ways to transform your marriage.

*Invite your husband to do the exercises in this book with you.* This is an excellent way to connect and spend quality time with each other. It is an opportunity for both of you to identify and fix any problems that are interfering with your marriage. Are you ready? Buckle up, hold on to your seat, and let's take this exciting journey together!

## Chapter 1

# The Woman

*Favour is deceitful, and beauty is vain: but a woman that feareth the Lord, she shall be praised.*
Proverbs 31:30 KJV

As women, we desire many things. We crave security, happiness, wealth, accountability, a sense of belonging, and a partner who can enhance or make us complete. We strongly believe that these needs will be fulfilled through a man.

For many reasons, most women's dream is to one day be married. From a tender age, many young girls have an idea of who they would like to marry. Some may fulfill their heart's desire, while some may end up with the opposite of who they were looking for. The fear of getting older, having no children, and still being single push many women to anxiously pursue marriage. Other reasons include the joy of being called "Mrs." and having the attention of a man while flashing their dazzling wedding ring. Some women are excellent nurturers and are looking for a man to nurture. Some refuse to remain alone and lonely, while some are simply intrigued by having a man to call their own. Lastly, many women say yes to marriage just to fulfill their sexual desires because it's *"better to marry than to burn"*(1 Corinthians 7:9).

Irrespective of why you want to get married, be sure he was chosen by God and not by your flesh. Perhaps you feel as if you are ready and should pursue marriage because all your friends and family members are married. Remember that God's timing is never wrong. When you wait patiently upon Him without interference, you will receive God's best. Do not miss receiving His perfect will and extraordinary blessings due to impatience.

While many singles are in the hot pursuit of marriage, many women who are married can't wait to be separated or divorced. Marriage is a lifetime commitment that requires hard work and dedication. What you enjoy doing now may become "a whip and a burden" after marriage because you will be doing the same things repeatedly—every day, 365 days a year. There are no vacations, no days off, no sick leave or PTO (Paid Time Off) in marriage. Therefore, never allow your flesh, friends, family, or even your pastor to push you into marriage prematurely. Think of it as horse racing. Once the horses go through the gate, there's no turning back. What you may see, feel, and call "love" may actually be infatuation or lust.

Some single women tend to put on a façade to impress the opposite sex. I say to you, my sister: Take off the mask! Pretending to be who you are not will unravel sooner than later, possibly causing a devastating effect and strain on the relationship. Failing to reveal all sides of your personality at the beginning of your relationship may disappoint you both. A woman may experience loneliness or divorce because her husband believes she has changed and refuses to tolerate the attitude and behavior she is exhibiting.

Being your authentic self gives the man a fair chance to choose if he wants to be with you for *who* you are. Stay consistent in your authenticity after marriage. How you spoke, conducted yourself, restrained your tongue, and checked your attitude during courtship should be maintained throughout your marriage. Remember, whatever you did that attracted him to you must continue. That way, your bond will become stronger as you grow together.

Upon meeting your potential husband, it is imperative to take things slowly. Take the time to assess his character, temperament, personality, and compatibility. When you decide to settle with your significant other, allow yourself to enjoy the relationship fully as you continue to learn about each other's likes, dislikes, and triggers. It is like a newborn baby; if you miss out on the first four years of their life, you've missed the best years, which can never be regained. You have missed the chance to bond and watch the baby as they grow and blossom into a beautiful child. *Furthermore, do not rush into marriage and bypass the bonding phase.* There are some things you should know before you say "I do" or engage in sexual activities. Have you heard the saying, "Familiarity breeds contempt?" Make sure you ask the relevant questions before you get too familiar with each other. Otherwise, you may never get answers to your unasked questions.

I know individuals who got married quickly without knowing anything about each other, and their marriages are still going strong after many years. However, in today's society, the odds of marrying unquestioningly and having a lasting relationship are exceptionally slim. To make a conscious and informed decision, spend quality time gathering as much information as possible about your prospective husband. Remember, though, that even though you make a significant effort getting to know him, the relationship can still collapse. Life is unpredictable. Nothing is guaranteed. May your discernment be your guide.

Beloved, never ignore the warning signs of a troubled future. Never try to convince yourself that he will change or that you can change him, and things will improve after marriage. Avoid choosing a mate simply because he is anointed and goes to church. If you select a man because of his outward appearance or accomplishments, you may ultimately be disappointed. Remember, the wedding only lasts a few hours, but marriage is a *lifetime commitment* accompanied by responsibilities, hard work, and major compromise. If you are willing to spend the rest of your lives together, do it with the spirit of excellence.

Be intentional about staying together regardless of any challenges you may face.

# Questionnaire

1. At what age did you think about marriage? Who did you dream of marrying? Did you get your heart's desire?

_____
_____
_____
_____
_____

2. Many women crave happiness, security, wealth, etc. What are/were you craving? Why?

_____
_____
_____
_____
_____

3. How well do you complement each other? What should you have done differently?

_____
_____
_____
_____
_____

4. What was your reason for wanting to get married?

_____
_____
_____
_____
_____
_____

5. What warning signs did you see but ignored because you believed he would change?

_____
_____
_____
_____
_____
_____

6. Was your husband chosen out of your flesh or was he directly sent by God?

_____
_____
_____
_____
_____
_____

7. How is your tongue getting in the way of your marriage?

8. Do you feel as if you have interfered with God's perfect will for your life by marrying this person?

9. How ready were you when you got married?

10. Many are getting divorced. What makes you believe that your marriage will stand the test of time?

_____
_____
_____
_____
_____
_____

11. How was the bonding period? Explain.

_____
_____
_____
_____
_____
_____

12. If you did not reveal the authentic you during courtship, how is it affecting your relationship now?

_____
_____
_____
_____
_____
_____

## Questionnaire

13. How can you tell if your husband is still attracted to you?

_____
_____
_____
_____
_____

14. Write your prayer pertaining to the subject at hand.

_____
_____
_____
_____
_____
_____
_____
_____
_____
_____
_____
_____
_____
_____

## Gliding on Cloud Nine

*Walk about Zion, and go round about her: tell the towers thereof. Mark ye well her bulwarks, consider her palaces; that ye may tell it to the generation following. For this God is our God forever and ever: He will be our guide even unto death.*
*Psalm 48:12-14 KJV*

According to scientists and meteorologists, "cloud nine" is the cirrus cloud, the highest cloud in the sky. However, I am not referring to the actual cloud in this context. I am referring to the overflowing, extreme state of bliss and happiness—that feeling of being on a high with excitement or ecstasy.

In the infancy stage of most relationships, individuals experience an unexplainable sense of belonging. At this point, they cannot imagine anything else other than being with each other. Before long, you may hear words such as these: "Honey, as I pondered about my future and where I see myself in five years, all I can see is obscurity without you. There can be no me without you in my life. Will you marry me?"

I can only imagine how you felt when you heard those melodious words uttered from the mouth of your significant other—the man of your dreams. I bet you felt as if you were floating on "cloud nine", blanketed in excitement and elation. As the weeks and months go by, you try to wrap your head around the thought of being a wife. With each move you make, it appears as if you are gliding in thin air. It may be hard for you to express what you are experiencing.

Beloved, the "cloud nine" experience is like an adrenaline rush; it will not last forever. As your floating on "cloud nine" comes to a screeching halt, prepare to face the reality of life. All that looked and felt stunningly beautiful to you during this gleeful period might irritate your spirit and cause you discomfort when the reality of married life settles in.

Nonetheless, do not succumb to despair or crumble under pressure when the rubber meets the road. I hope you will never use the word "regret" to describe your experience. On gloomy days, I encourage you to reflect on the days filled with laughter and happiness. Remember the days when you were inseparable. Think of the times when you felt like nothing could go wrong, interfere with that blissful feeling, or deter you from marrying your chosen man. It is essential to take things slowly and continually assess the situation as you embark upon your married journey.

# Questionnaire

1. Describe how you felt when your husband asked you to marry him.

___

2. List five things that made you feel as if you were floating on "cloud nine."

___

3. Elaborate on your "cloud nine" days.

___

4. What does it feel like to be on "cloud nine?"

_____
_____
_____
_____
_____

5. Now that the "cloud nine" days have ended, what areas of your marriage need polishing?

_____
_____
_____
_____
_____

6. "Cloud nine" experiences tend to vanish in real life. How do you plan to cope with real-life issues?

_____
_____
_____
_____
_____

7. How do you plan to overcome the gloomy days?

_____
_____
_____
_____
_____
_____

8. What are some of the questions you have asked yourself during the "cloud nine" experience?

_____
_____
_____
_____
_____
_____

9. Comparing your "cloud nine" days to the present, what is your preference and why?

_____
_____
_____
_____
_____
_____

10. Write a prayer pertaining to the subject at hand.

## The Adorning

*I decked thee also with ornaments, and I put bracelets upon thy hands, and a chain on thy neck. And I put a jewel on thy forehead, and earrings in thine ears, and a beautiful crown upon thine head. Thus wast thou decked with gold and silver; and thy raiment was of fine linen, and silk, and broidered work; thou didst eat fine flour, and honey, and oil: and thou wast exceeding beautiful, and thou didst prosper into a kingdom. And thy renown went forth among the heathen for thy beauty:*
*for it was perfect through my comeliness,*
*which I had put upon thee, saith the Lord GOD.*
*Ezekiel 16:11-14 KJV*

Single women seeking a mate tend to put extra effort into self-care and how they adorn themselves. Their hair or wig is always in place and if they wear makeup, it is perfectly applied. Nothing is wrong with making an extra effort in self-care and expressing your beauty. As a kingdom woman, you not only represent yourself when you are elegantly attired; you also represent your heavenly Father, God. Unfortunately, some women believe that beauty means wearing revealing or tight-fitting clothing and will increase their chances of attracting a husband. Men will stare at a woman wearing tight or revealing outfits, but perhaps not from the intent the woman desires; instead, they may stare lustfully. Some men may stare in disgust, wondering why she is exposing so much.

My sister, I encourage you to apply wisdom and use discretion when attracting the opposite sex. You can't go wrong dressing modestly. As strange as it may seem, most men are attracted to elegance and class more than to sensuality. So, try not to overdo it or reveal too much; you may chase away your potential husband.

One of the biggest mistakes women make after marriage is to let themselves go physically. Their essential self-care declines or is ignored altogether. No more emphasis is placed on their appearance as they stroll around the house with uncombed hair and a huge housedress. Elegance has taken a back seat, and makeup and personal hygiene are no longer on their priority list.

Beloved, staying refined and elegant *after* marriage is just as important as before the wedding. In fact, more *effort* should be put into refining your body and your appearance. Keep it simple yet beautiful. Never assume that because you are married, your husband will accept or be comfortable with you taking less care of yourself. Once again, men are drawn to physical attraction; therefore, your husband will continue looking forward to seeing his wife attractively adorned.

Sadly, some women are explicitly attracted to married men and will go above and beyond to arrest their attention. Do not be naïve; your husband is not exempt. Therefore, present yourself in a way that will keep your husband's mind lingering on you throughout the day. Knowing he has a classy and elegant woman at home will go a long way in deterring him from yielding to the temptations or lust of another woman's seductive behaviors. Keep the excitement in the air, and do not lose your attractiveness. Stay beautiful inside and out, my sister.

# Questionnaire

1. In your own words, define what it means to adorn oneself.

_____
_____
_____
_____
_____
_____

2. What did you do to capture your husband's attention?

_____
_____
_____
_____
_____
_____

3. How do you plan to maintain your husband's attraction toward you?

_____
_____
_____
_____
_____
_____
_____
_____

4. What is your view on women of God who wear tight-fitting, short, and revealing clothing in public or in church?

_____
_____
_____
_____
_____
_____
_____

5. Can you sincerely say that the way you attire represents and pleases God and the public at large? If not, what are you going to do about it?

_____
_____
_____
_____
_____
_____
_____

6. Have you heard any complaints or negative comments about the way you attire? If so, what are they?

_____
_____
_____
_____
_____
_____
_____

7. Based on your attire, can someone look at you and say, "There goes a child of God/Christian"?

_____
_____
_____
_____
_____
_____

8. List several ways you can nonverbally persuade your husband to remain desirous of you.

_____
_____
_____
_____
_____
_____

9. What does the bible says about how a woman should attire?

_____
_____
_____
_____
_____
_____

10. How comfortable are you with the way you attire yourself?

_____
_____
_____
_____
_____
_____
_____

11. How should a kingdom woman attire herself as an ambassador of God?

_____
_____
_____
_____
_____
_____
_____

12. I do not believe that your choice of clothing will keep you out of heaven or send you to hell. However, do you think there should be an identifier for kingdom representation versus worldly representation? Please elaborate.

_____
_____
_____
_____
_____
_____
_____

13. Write about any experience you may have in this area. Create a prayer pertaining to this topic.

# Freedom

*There is difference also between a wife and a virgin. The unmarried woman careth for the things of the Lord, that she may be holy both in body and in spirit: but she that is married careth for the things of the world, how she may please her husband.*
*1 Corinthians 7:34 KJV*

Do you know that there are women who are happily single? Yes, and they are genuinely comfortable in this role, loving and cherishing themselves. Freedom can be a woman's best friend. Being single means you are free to do whatever you choose, whenever you choose. You can travel the world with extended stays if you desire. You can invite friends over for dinner, go out for lunch dates, and occasionally enjoy a girls' night out.

Being single has many other benefits as well, such as sleeping in, not worrying about waking up to make breakfast or being asked, "What's for lunch or dinner?" One of the most rewarding benefits of being single is the freedom and ability to spend more time with God while basking in His presence without interruption. This freedom in being single allows you to be more connected to God, fostering spiritual growth as you seek to please Him.

Your marital status does not determine your gifting, calling, or your level of spirituality. It is crucial to realize that your single life is a precious time for personal growth and exploration. Marriage, when it comes, should be a choice made with confidence and certainty. After marriage, life will not only be about you; it will be about your spouse and children, if any. And if you are a *pastor's wife*, it will be about your spouse, children, and the church!

Ponder this: you may not be as free to do all the fun things you did as a single woman. You are now accountable to your husband, who has become your covering (Ephesians 5:22-25) and should be your priority. However, if you are the type of woman who will tell your husband, "I don't feel like it, and I'm not doing it," "I don't like a man telling me what to do," or "Do it yourself," my friend, hold on to your freedom. You are definitely *not* ready for marriage. It is important to remember that marriage is a partnership, not a burden. It requires readiness, understanding, and the willingness to compromise.

Being married means being your spouse's help-meet. Ephesians 5:22-25 instructs you to be submissive and obedient to your husband, which shows respect and humility for him and the future of the marriage. These values are not about losing your freedom, but about building a strong and respectful relationship. If you believe he is not worth losing your freedom for, do not waste your or his time. Avoid leading him to think that all is well, while deep within, you view him as a weak link and a pushover.

Embrace your freedom. Enjoy it while it lasts, and then embrace your marriage fully.

## Questionnaire

1. What do you miss about your freedom?

___

2. What are your regrets, if any?

___

3. Who do you spend more time with, your husband or God? How do you plan to create a balance?

___

4. Are you behaving as if you are still single and independent? If so, how is this affecting your marriage?

_____
_____
_____
_____
_____
_____

5. Now that you are married, do you feel he is worth giving up your freedom? Elaborate.

_____
_____
_____
_____
_____
_____

6. What is it about your marriage that makes you happy to forget about your single days of freedom?

_____
_____
_____
_____
_____
_____
_____

7. How often do you find yourself wishing you were single?

_____
_____
_____
_____
_____
_____
_____

8. If you knew before marriage what you know now, what would you have done differently?

_____
_____
_____
_____
_____
_____
_____

9. What do you like about sharing your life with your partner?

_____
_____
_____
_____
_____
_____
_____

10. True or False: Freedom is a woman's worst nightmare.

11. Write your prayer pertaining to this topic.

## Discernment

*Beloved, believe not every spirit, but try the spirits whether they are of God: because many false prophets are gone out into the world.*
*1 John 4:1 KJV*

Discernment. Some call it "unction," and some refer to it as "something tells me." To some, "it's a feeling I can't shake." Some call it "insight," while others call it "a gut feeling." When your spiritual discernment is activated, you will know or see things not visible to the physical eyes. You are equipped to identify good and evil through the Holy Spirit and empowered to foresee hidden dangers and agendas, giving you a profound sense of confidence and capability.

For instance, you may be standing in a room filled with people, yet you can identify those who are there for selfish reasons and those with sincere motives. Further, an individual may approach you and say the most flattering and encouraging words, but immediately, your spirit discerns that those are empty words. Their words are not coming from the heart; you may even discern that the individual dislikes you.

Many times, we fall prey to Satan and his agents because we lack the spirit of discernment. We readily open doors for the wolves to enter our secret place because we have mistaken them for sheep. For far too long, God's people have suffered hurt, disappointment, and sometimes death because they lacked *discernment*. This realization should make us more cautious and alert, understanding the paramount importance of spiritual discernment in avoiding deception. This heightened awareness should prepare us to face the challenges of discernment.

Do you know that the anointing on your life can attract the good, bad, and ugly? Men and women may gravitate to you because of your anointing. Some would like to be your covering to protect you from the vultures. Some may want to teach you how to polish or hone your gifts to prepare you for the next level of assignment. Some may perceive you as a great value to their ministry and believe you can do mighty exploits for the Lord. Some will come flashing their titles, flaunting how they can introduce you to people in high places, and bragging about how far they can propel you and your ministry. It is imperative to discern the true motivations behind these actions, as it empowers you to make informed decisions and take responsibility for your relationships.

Do not be frightened or get carried away with the titles of pastor, evangelist, apostle, teacher, prophet, bishop, or doctor. *Activate your discernment, be vigilant, and observe the movement of those around you.* Even though it appears they want the best for you and to enhance your ministry, it may not be so. Their mouths could be uttering one thing while their hearts are screaming something else. Avoid being broadsided by the spirit of manipulation and deception. Once again, activate your discernment. This reminder should motivate and encourage you to be more discerning in your interactions.

Unfortunately, there are so-called men and women of God who are opportunists. They will approach you with "great concern" about your well-being but with a self-serving motive. Their desire is not to push or groom you to become a better person. Instead, they intend to ride on your anointing, meet your acquaintances, stand on your platform to build their own, and boost their ego at *your* expense to promote themselves. Wasting no time, they will quickly attach themselves to your established ministry. Before you know it, you are shoved to the back burner through the spirits of deception and manipulation as they try to take over. At this point, you are being ordered around, being told what, where, when, and how to do your assignment by the same individuals who pretended they had your best interests at heart.

Fasting to receive or reactivate the spirit of discernment should be your priority. Ask God to sharpen your discernment so you can identify and analyze your prospects, whether in marriage or business. Do not forget that not all that glitters is gold. My sister, please train your spirit to search the heart and intention of an individual before your flesh falls or becomes attached to him. Beware of wolves adorned in sheep's clothing who come to accomplish their hidden agenda of stripping you of your gifts and anointing. In the name of Jesus, I command your spiritual eyes to be opened now.

# Questionnaire

1. On a scale of 1–10, how strong is your discernment?

_____
_____
_____
_____
_____
_____

2. What are some aspects or situations you were able to discern, but can't anymore?

_____
_____
_____
_____
_____
_____

3. Have you ever been taken off guard because you failed to discern? How will you make sure it doesn't happen again?

_____
_____
_____
_____
_____
_____

4. In your own words, define "discernment" and its importance.

___

5. Can you recall anyone who approached you as an angel of light, but was like a wolf in sheep's clothing? If so, what was their motive and how did you handle it?

___

6. Have you ever been approached by an opportunist? If so, how vulnerable were you? What was your response or reaction?

___

7. Can you identify anyone around you who wants to ride on your anointing and your platform for fame? If yes, how do you prepare to fight that battle?

_____
_____
_____
_____
_____
_____

8. When your husband proposed marriage, what did you sense about him in your spirit?

_____
_____
_____
_____
_____
_____

9. What is your plan to regain and maintain your sense of discernment?

_____
_____
_____
_____
_____
_____
_____

10. What devastation have you suffered due to lost or unused discernment?

_____
_____
_____
_____
_____
_____
_____

11. How do you identify with this passage?

_____
_____
_____
_____
_____
_____
_____

12. Write your prayer pertaining to this theme.

_____
_____
_____
_____
_____
_____
_____
_____

## Chapter 2

# The Wife

*Therefore shall a man leave his father and his mother, and shall cleave unto his wife: and they shall be one flesh.*
*Genesis 2:24 KJV*

You do not need a PhD or a degree to become a wife. Being a wife is an honorable and prestigious position, especially when God handpicked you for that particular individual. I like to use acronyms to explain my thoughts. Here is my interpretation of a wife in acronym form:

**W** - Woman of wisdom
**I** - Intercessor
**F** - Firm
**E** - Entertain/Engage

### Wisdom

*If any of you lacks wisdom, you should ask God, who gives generously to all without finding fault, and it will be given to you.*
*James 1:5 NIV*

As a kingdom wife, you are expected to exercise wisdom in every area, especially when approaching your husband about sensitive subjects. This wisdom empowers you to be in control and to make life-altering decisions that may negatively affect your marriage. If you are married to a pastor, he has to counsel, advise, mentor, and pray for others. Therefore, remember that he will spend extensive time with male and female church members. In that scenario, I encourage you to exercise godly wisdom, cast down any negative imaginations, and rebuke the spirit of jealousy.

It is a reality that you will share your husband with the congregation and the neighborhood. Reacting with negative words toward your husband is a clear sign of a lack of wisdom. If necessary, pray for self-control and the ability to restrain your tongue from speaking offensively.

Seeking God's wisdom is vital to preserving and protecting your marriage, character, and dignity. Each time you pray, ask Him to endow you with His wisdom. This applied wisdom will draw your husband's heart a little closer to you each day, giving you reassurance and confidence in your decision-making.

> *The wise woman builds her house, but with her own hands*
> *the foolish one tears hers down.*
> Proverbs 14:1 NIV

## Intercessor

An intercessor differs from someone who loves to pray and may pray basic or general prayers. This person selflessly takes on the burden of others and brings them to the Lord through relentless prayer. As an intercessor, you stand in the gap for individuals. You labor intensely to battle their spiritual warfare, fighting for the spiritual and physical freedom of those you know and even those you don't know. Intercessory prayer is not a ten or fifteen-minute prayer but a longer commitment.

As your husband's personal intercessor, you negotiate through prayer for his safety, ministry, mind, and life. You are his negotiator and mediator, standing between him and the wiles and fiery darts of the enemy. Due to his spiritual responsibility, assignment, burden, and confidential matters of the church, extensive intercessions and coverings are needed.

## Firm

For a healthy and peaceful marriage, compromise may be necessary on occasion—depending on the situation. It is important to remember that compromise is not a sign of weakness, but a strength that can enhance your relationship. However, there are moments when you must stand firm and defend the truth, righteousness, and holiness. With love and humility, be respectfully unwavering against anything contrary to the Word of God.

Keep your firm conviction about what is right without compromising your character and integrity. If your husband is inclined to engage in a situation that may be detrimental to his walk and ministry, firmly deter him. Without being bossy or a bully, firmly explain the ramifications of walking outside God's perfect will and the consequences of not wearing his full armor.

Being firm does not mean usurping authority or rebelling against your husband's requests. It also doesn't mean being rude, prideful, or self-centered. You can be firm without being bossy, which means you can express your opinions and concerns in a respectful and assertive manner, without being controlling or domineering.

### Entertain and Engage

Never miss the opportunity to put a smile on your husband's face. With his tight and sometimes stressful schedule and overwhelming responsibilities, your role in creating joyful experiences is super important. It will be thoughtful of you to create some form of entertainment to stimulate and help him maintain a sound mind, showing him how much you care for and love him.

Entertainment can take many forms, from a surprise candlelight dinner of his favorite meal to engaging in mind-stimulating board games, trivias, or puzzles. Sprinkle flower petals around the tub and on the bed and fill the air with joyful music. These shared activities not only entertain but also foster a sense of connection and engagement. Enjoy each other's company in a way that suits both of your preferences.

## Being a Pastor's Wife

*Whoso findeth a wife findeth a good thing,
and obtaineth favour of the Lord.
Proverbs 18:22 KJV*

The role of a pastor's wife is a unique journey of on-the-job training. It is a path that no one can fully prepare you for, and it doesn't come with a manual. This uniqueness is what makes it so special and valuable.

Not every woman is a wife, but every wife is a woman. Proverbs 31:10-30, a passage in which a woman is often referred to as the "virtuous woman" or "Proverbs 31 woman," provides a biblical framework for the role of a kingdom wife. It defines what a kingdom wife should do and how she should behave and care for her husband. Wives should be virtuous—having or showing high moral standards while exhibiting a spirit of excellence.

Looking back on the above-mentioned Scripture, a wife is priceless. She makes her husband her priority. He is pampered and well cared for, so there should be no reason for him to go astray. Her thoughts toward him are pure, and she is always looking for ways to honor and appease him.

*Being a Pastor's Wife*

A wife's role in the family is of the utmost importance. She ensures that her family is well-fed, comfortable, and nurtured. She does everything in her power to make her family look good and feel safe, loved, honored, and respected. This integral role is what makes her a cornerstone of her family.

A ruby is known for its beauty, attributes, and durability. These gem stones are not found near or on surfaces. Rubies are between three to twenty-four meters (9.843–78.7402 feet) deep within rocks, and some are found on ocean floors. Comparing a kingdom wife to this precious stone signifies that they are rare and unique. You will not find them in most places; therefore, you must search for them. Like a ruby, kingdom wives have unique characteristics that cannot be hidden. You, as a kingdom wife, are a rare gem, cherished and valued.

As a pastor's wife, you are chosen to make your husband feel special and arouse the king in him. The treatment you give your husband must be exclusive—completely different from how you treat others. This exclusivity is a testament to his importance in your life. When the king in him is aroused, he will treat you like a queen and sing your praises according to Proverbs 10:28. Always seek to minister to his needs emotionally, mentally, spiritually, and physically.

Avoid being mentored or influenced by women on how to treat your husband if they are not married or while their marriages are in turmoil, and they refuse to work on them or give grace to their husbands. Whatever he is not doing, address it with him privately and leave it in the hands of God. Following the instruction or advice of these women may cause you to neglect your wifely duties and ruin an excellent relationship. Some good can be found in everyone, irrespective of their shortcomings.

There will be moments when you feel unappreciated and that the enemy is breathing down your neck, softly whispering, "You are being used." As a result, you stop doing what God expects you to do for your husband. Perhaps you start murmuring and complaining that these are modern days, and you are nobody's "gal" or slave. He has two hands; he can do it, too. But remember, sister, you are not just a helper, you are a vital part of his ministry. Your worth is immeasurable, and your role is irreplaceable.

Have you ever wondered why God has given you this specific task? If you're in a professional role, such as a secretary, you know the importance of following your job description. But what if you decided to stop answering the phone, ignore emails, and not respond to any correspondence? You could choose to do so, but what would the consequences be? Similarly, what happens to your relationship when you disregard God's plan for your marriage and refuse to follow His guidance?

Some people believe that a pastor's wife always wears big hats, high heels, and long tailored suits, and that she is the first person in church on Sunday or Sabbath morning, sitting in the front row. Some also believe that she must have a smile and a sophisticated look every day of the year. While others think she should work in all departments and never miss a church service. However, behind these expectations, there are personal struggles that pastors' wives often face. Some pastors' wives may feel like they do not fit in or that they are not accepted.

Beloved, always remember that you are a human being first, and then a pastor's wife. Your sense of self, purpose, and identity should never be overshadowed by tradition or stigmas. You are not here to please everyone, and that's okay. You don't need to fit into any societal mold. Be comfortable in your own skin and represent your Father well. You are the pastor's wife, not the wife of the church. Your first assignment from God is to serve your husband to the best of your ability (Ephesians 5:22).

In addition, remember that you automatically became your husband's personal counselor, mentor, therapist, psychiatrist, cheerleader, encourager, and best friend when you married him. You get to observe the man of God in his element when he is under the anointing and being used mightily by God. You will share the moments when he is in an excellent mood and walking on "cloud nine". Unfortunately, you will also experience the moments when he is frightened, vulnerable, in pain, heartbroken, silent for a long time, or ready to quit the ministry.

Wife, your role is crucial. You have a challenging yet vital job to perform. These are the moments when you must put on your counseling hat and minister to your spouse's mind, heart, soul, and spirit. Your support is not just important, it is invaluable. Sometimes, you need to use your discernment to analyze the situation. Does he need to be left alone, spoken to, or given a lingering hug without uttering a word? Your actions can make a significant difference. Sometimes, he will do better simply with the ministry of presence. (Therefore, be present but say nothing.)

Prepare your mind to adjust and embrace numerous changes, especially when hanging out randomly with your lady friends or sitting back and doing nothing. Most of your weekends will be occupied with being a help-meet to your husband, which should be your priority. As his wife and first lady, you will assist him with many church duties, especially for his Sabbath or Sunday morning services. Please do not misunderstand what I am saying. Your life is not over. Learning how to manage your time well is crucial. It will determine how you spend your downtime to prevent burnout, overwhelming feelings, hatred for the ministry, and resentment toward your husband. It will also give you a sense of control and empowerment.

As mentioned before, a few of your primary duties as his wife are interceding and covering your husband/pastor. Before and after he mounts the pulpit, position yourself to pray, covering the man of God with the blood of Jesus. After delivering a powerful sermon, he is vulnerable to the enemy's attack. At these times, you need to lay hands on him while you pray and minister to his spirit and flesh, knowing that your prayers are powerful and effective in supporting his ministry.

There will be occasions when your husband will be invited to minister in various places, and you will be unable to accompany him. Nevertheless, stay on your knees and intercede for him while he is away. Here is a great strategy: Ask your husband when he is scheduled to bring the Word. Then, rally a group of trusted members to pray with you on his behalf while he is preaching.

Dear woman of God, it is crucial to be vigilant against the enemy's tactics that aim to undermine God's work through His vessel. Refrain from becoming a tool in Satan's hands to tear down your husband, especially in public. If you have concerns about his sermon, his lengthy conversations with members, or his failure to acknowledge you from the pulpit, remember that these matters are best discussed in private. Your husband deserves your respect and privacy when addressing his shortcomings. Be diplomatic in your approach when pointing out his failures and flaws. Never correct him in the presence of anyone else. Please do not allow him to feel insignificant, inferior, stupid, or incompetent. He is not your child but your partner, your equal, and the head of the house. What if you were in his position? How and where would you like him to handle the situation?

It is essential to be sensitive to your husband's feelings. Resist and rebuke any attempts by Satan to use you against your husband. By fostering a supportive and understanding relationship, you can help protect your husband from the influence of domineering, controlling, and wicked spirits. Your empathy and care can be a powerful shield against negative influences. This compassionate approach will strengthen your bond and create a safe haven for your husband.

As a cheerleader and encourager of your husband, remember that you play a crucial role in his life. It's imperative to reassure him that he means the world to you. Show him how much you appreciate him and tell him he is your champion and mentor. Those words from his partner will boost his morale and strengthen your relationship. Your role as his cheerleader is not to be underestimated. Your support and encouragement can be a beacon of light in his life, uplifting him in his journey as a pastor.

I heard of a story in which the pastor's wife verbally attacked him immediately after he dismissed the church service. With an elevated voice, she began a temper tantrum about how long he spent talking to church members, knowing she had to go to work the following day. Satan got a hold of her and began using her as a tool to crush her husband's ego. She belittled him in the presence of church members and visitors. The pastor's face showed a mix of shame, embarrassment, and a profound loss of joy and peace of mind that revealed his heavy emotional burden. If the earth opened up and swallowed him in that moment, perhaps he would rejoice.

Continue to be each other's cheerleaders.

# Questionnaire

1. What have you learned from this passage?

_____
_____
_____
_____
_____
_____

2. How will you apply what you have learned?

_____
_____
_____
_____
_____
_____

3. Describe what you felt when you first got married and woke up as a pastor's wife.

_____
_____
_____
_____
_____
_____

4. In what way(s) does your marriage meet or not meet your expectations? Is there a wrestling within your spirit concerning if he is the right one?

_____
_____
_____
_____
_____
_____
_____

5. Given the current situation, what would you do differently?

_____
_____
_____
_____
_____
_____
_____

6. Are you enjoying your role as a pastor's wife? Why or why not?

_____
_____
_____
_____
_____
_____
_____

7. According to the passage above, which spirits should you bind up when praying and why?

_____
_____
_____
_____
_____

8. Were you ready for marriage when you said yes? Or who were you trying to please?

_____
_____
_____
_____
_____

9. Were you hoping that someone else would ask you for your hand in marriage instead of your current husband?

_____
_____
_____
_____
_____

10. During courtship, what "stop signs" did you observe but were determined to run through anyway?

_____
_____
_____
_____
_____
_____
_____

11. How do you plan to handle his vulnerable moments? How do you plan to celebrate his wins?

_____
_____
_____
_____
_____
_____
_____

12. True or False: There is a training manual on how to be a pastor's wife.

13. Have you identified ways to enhance the ministries within the church?

_____
_____
_____
_____
_____

14. Write your prayer pertaining to this theme.

_____
_____
_____
_____
_____
_____
_____
_____
_____
_____
_____
_____
_____
_____
_____

## Love God's Way

*Above all, love each other deeply,
because love covers over a multitude of sins.
1Peter 4:8 NIV*

*"Jesus, I love you. I adore you. Lord, you are the lover of my soul. Lord, my heart belongs to you; you are my heartbeat and the bishop of my soul. Father, there is nothing I wouldn't do for you. Use me as you please."*

Are these the words we express during prayer to our heavenly Father?

It is thought-provoking how we profess our unwavering love for God yet struggle to extend the same love to our life partners. The term "I love you" is often easily used but is not always unconditional. Regrettably, many of us tend to show love only to those who are compliant, submissive, and humble—those who are easily swayed. Conversely, we often find it challenging to love those we cannot control—the assertive, outspoken, and self-assured individuals.

Let us explore the profound insights of the ancient Greeks, who categorized love into eight distinct types. These words, each with its unique meaning, provide us with a comprehensive understanding of love from diverse perspectives.

- ***Eros*** or erotic love: The kind of love that describes sexual desire or passion between a man and a woman.
- ***Mania*** or obsessive love: In this type of love, the individual becomes codependent on their partner, believing that they can't survive without that person. If the individual feels like he or she is not being loved in the same manner, they can become violent and destructive.
- ***Ludus*** or playful love: This kind of love is shared between young lovers during the early stage of courtship.
- ***Storge*** or familial love: This is the nurturing form of love between parents and their children.
- ***Philia*** or affectionate love: This refers to casual yet genuine friendship, without physical or sexual attraction. It is also known as a platonic relationship.
- ***Agape*** love: This is the unconditional, everlasting, divine love expressed between God and man.
- ***Pragma*** or enduring love: This is a uniquely mature type of love that withstands the test of time. It is cultivated simultaneously by both husband and wife in order to keep their relationship alive.
- ***Philautia*** or self-love: This is not a prideful, self-centered, or selfish kind of love, but one that urges you to pay extra attention to your physical and spiritual well-being. Love yourself enough to be mindful of the things you eat and of your appearance. Love yourself enough to ensure that you are getting adequate sleep and rest.

Love is not just a feeling, it is a choice. Jesus sets the perfect example of intentional love and how to love each other His way. Loving your husband God's way should not be a casual experience but a deliberate endeavor regardless of how you feel about him or how dissatisfied you are with his behavior. The love of God is pure, without grudge, never-ending, and honest. Loving your husband God's way means choosing to overlook his mistakes, shortcomings, bad habits, and ugly patterns—just as Jesus did for you and me.

My sister, perhaps life at home is not desirable, and you are faced with unfavorable situations in which loving your husband God's way is extremely difficult. Nevertheless, think about your soul and ways to please God, not your flesh. Remember, God did not wait for us to choose His Son Jesus as our Lord and Savior or for us to become perfect before He surrendered His life for humanity. Though undeserving of His love and mercy, He expressed unconditional love, redeeming us from hell, death, and the grave. Despite our sinful, wicked nature, and our being enemies of the cross, He did not hesitate to extend authentic love toward the human race. For the sake of your soul and destiny, think continuously about selflessness and sacrifice. Unquestionably, your husband's actions will provoke you at some point during your relationship, so much so that you may contemplate walking away from the marriage. In such instances, think long and hard about your sacred vows before God and man. Can you recall the moments when you were not at your best and disappointed God? Yet, He never gave you the silent treatment or walked away. Instead, God woke you up every morning, prolonged your life, and honored you with new mercy daily.

When you express sincere love toward your husband and make it a way of life, you will attract God's attention and move His hands to defend your marriage, ministry, finances, and salvation. This should motivate and encourage you to work harder on loving your husband as God commands. Remember, whatever you do, do it as unto the Lord. Your rewards, blessings, and promotions all come from God. When you allow God to reign in your heart, your actions, words, thoughts, and behaviors will be transformed, and you will feel free to love the unlovable. Your treatment of your husband is a direct reflection of your relationship with Jesus Christ. Consider this deeply.

What are you thinking? What kinds of thoughts are flowing through your mind that you need to take captive and render obedient to Christ? Perhaps if you search deep in your heart, you may find a strong dislike for your husband because of how he treats you. He may fail to express his love for you and show appreciation for all you have done. Nonetheless, avoid complaining to others about what he is not doing or how much you have done for him, which he never reciprocates. Even though he is not fulfilling his duty, God will not condone you discussing and demeaning your husband with strangers. I encourage you to seek counseling as you continue to fulfill your role as his wife, help-meet, and friend.

*Casting down imaginations, and every high thing that exalteth itself against the knowledge of God, and bringing into captivity every thought to the obedience of Christ*
1 Cointhians 10:5 KJV

*If a man say, I love God, and hateth his brother, he is a liar: for he that loveth not his brother whom he hath seen, how can he love God whom he hath not seen?*
1 John 4:20 KJV

# Questionnaire

1. Define "love" in your own words.
   _____
   _____
   _____
   _____
   _____
   _____

2. How would you classify the love that you have for your husband?
   _____
   _____
   _____
   _____
   _____
   _____

3. Do you love him God's way or are you only tolerating him? Explain.
   _____
   _____
   _____
   _____
   _____
   _____

4. From the passage, give the meaning to each of these words listed below.

Eros

Mania

Ludus

Storge

Philia

Agape

_____
_____
_____

Pragma

_____
_____
_____

Philautia

_____
_____
_____

5. How do you plan to deal with your husband's annoyance?

_____
_____
_____
_____
_____
_____

6. True or False: It would be best to divorce your husband when he vexes your spirit and annoys your flesh.

7. Complete the following. Loving your husband God's way means you will:

___

8. True or False: Loving someone God's way should not be a casual experience, but an intentional endeavor regardless of how you feel about the individual.

9. What are the consequences of resentment, unforgiveness, and hate?

___

10. Write out this Scripture twice: 1 John 4:20-21 KJV

_____
_____
_____
_____
_____
_____

11. On a blank piece of paper, draw a vertical line in the center. On one side, list the unfavorable aspects of your husband. On the other side, list the good things about him. From this list, highlight a few of his admirable traits, and then express to him how appreciative you are of those specific qualities. Tell him exactly why you are grateful, as it can give him a different perspective on you and the relationship.

12. Write your prayer pertaining to the subject at hand.

_____
_____
_____
_____
_____
_____
_____
_____

## Do Not Let Your Temper Control You

*Know this, my beloved brothers: let every person be quick to hear, slow to speak, slow to anger.*
*James 1:19 ESV*

If I asked your husband how he feels about the marriage, would he be elated to share his satisfaction and express his gratitude for you as a treasure? Would he sing your praises, declaring that you are the best thing that ever happened to him? Or would he express misery and discontentment? Would he vent about how uncomfortable and tired he is of your continuous temper tantrums, disrespect, and flare-ups at the slightest disagreement?

As the Scripture reminds us, "It is better to dwell on a corner of the roof than in the house with a quarrelsome wife" (Proverbs 21:9 NIV). A lack of self-control can be a deal breaker in any relationship, let alone marriage. Anger gives way to the enemy to intervene and put a wedge between you and your husband. It opens the doors to other sinful behaviors that will lead toward a rift in your relationship—not only with your husband, but with God forever *unless* repentance and forgiveness take place.

When the situation reaches the point of you becoming verbally abusive, think back on your salvation. Analyze your actions and then ask yourself: *Is this the character of a born-again believer? Is the Lord really satisfied with my attitude?* Uncontrolled temper and anger are disruptive and destructive. When you feel the urge to lash out or respond aggressively to your husband, pause and breathe deeply. Then, ask God to give you His peace and temperance. Take control of the spirit of anger before it controls you. Use the following Scriptures to comfort your mind and quell the spirit of anger: Ephesians 4:26, 31, Psalm 37:8, and Proverbs 15:1.

Have you heard the saying, *"Sticks and stones will break my bones, but words can never hurt me"*?

That is so far from the truth. Negative words can create deep wounds that may take a life-time to heal. Their scars may manifest through ungodly behavior and lingering discomfort and pain, whether physical, mental, or emotional. On the flip side, positive words have the power to heal, inspire, and uplift. They create a bond that strengthens over time, fostering a relationship built on trust, love, and understanding.

As a kingdom woman, make an extra effort to control your emotions instead of them controlling you. The harsher the words you hurl at your husband, the farther he may drift away from you emotionally, mentally, and physically. It is unhealthy to live in a marriage in which one or both spouses are like ticking time bombs. Think carefully about your words before you speak. Spoken words cannot be retracted.

If your temper is the first thing your husband sees, he may never get to know the real you. He may never experience your excellent attributes or extraordinary potential. Center your marriage around James 1:19.

It will make a huge difference when you listen without interruption, think before you respond, and reject and rebuke anger. If you struggle with anger, seek deliverance through prayer and fasting, along with professional help.

Keep in mind that seeking help is not a sign of weakness but a testament to your strength and commitment to your marriage. If you find yourself struggling with anger, know that there are resources and professionals who can guide you toward a healthier, more fulfilling relationship.

## Questionnaire

1. How would you describe your temper during heated conversations or when you're disappointed?

___

2. How is your temper affecting marriage?

___

3. Do your mouth and tongue need restraint? Explain.

___

4. Identify what triggers your anger.

_____
_____
_____
_____
_____
_____

5. How do you plan to keep your temper under control? ?

_____
_____
_____
_____
_____
_____

6. Now that you have identified the things that make you angry, how do you plan to fix them?

_____
_____
_____
_____
_____
_____

7. Can you honestly say that your husband knows the extraordinary you? Has he met the real you?

_____
_____
_____
_____
_____
_____
_____

8. List your weaknesses and how you are going to work on them.

_____
_____
_____
_____
_____
_____
_____

9. What are your strengths? How do you plan to enhance and maintain them?

_____
_____
_____
_____
_____
_____
_____

10. What do you think your husband would say about this chapter?

___

11. *Write the following sentence three times:* "If my temper is the first thing my husband sees, he will never get to know the real me or experience my excellent attributes or extraordinary potential."

___

12. Write out these verses: Ephesians 4:26, 31, and 32; Psalm 37:8; and Proverbs 15:1.

___

13. Write your prayer pertaining to the subject at hand.

## Say Goodbye to Ego and Pride

*Let not the foot of pride come against me,
and let not the hand of the wicked remove me.
Psalm 36:11 KJV*

It may present a problem for an independent woman to suddenly become submissive to her husband because her ego and pride may stand in the way of humility. Nevertheless, keep reminding yourself that you are no longer a single woman, and that you have now invited a man to share your life. This can be shown through simple acts of respect, such as listening to his opinions without interrupting, considering his feelings before making decisions, and compromising on decisions that are important to him. The moment you said, "I do," you traded the words *I, me, mine and my, for us, we, and ours.*

Unchecked pride and ego may cause you to use your intellect, financial stability and other accomplishments to sabotage your marriage. The spirit of pride will tutor you to treat your husband as one beneath you, while ego will influence you to see yourself as his superior and lifeline. Pride will also make you rebel against your husband's suggestions or ideas, especially if he is not as accomplished as you are. However, prioritizing respect and understanding in the relationship can prevent these behaviors and lead to a stronger bond.

Pride, by its self-exalting nature, often reveals itself just before it inflicts its destructive blow. Understanding the spirit of pride is crucial. It manifests when you display arrogance, selfishness, and excessive self-promotion. Also, idolizing one's self and placing it on a pedestal while belittling others is the manifestation of pride at work. Being aware of these traits empowers you to destroy pride and its destructive influence. Recognizing and combating the spirits of pride and ego should be a priority in pursuing a successful marriage. A long, successful marriage filled with humility, love, and respect is a powerful force that can paralyze those spirits. The absence of pride will result in a happy marriage and a genuine relationship with your heavenly Father and make you more pliable in the hands of God. Remember, "you" are history and have been replaced by "us." Pride exalts itself just before it destroys its victim, but humility is the key to a deep, inspiring spiritual connection.

*When pride cometh, then cometh shame:*
*but with the lowly is wisdom.*
*Proverbs 11:2 KJV*

# Questionnaire

1. How is pride affecting your marriage?

_____
_____
_____
_____
_____
_____

2. List several ways that you can overcome pride.

_____
_____
_____
_____
_____
_____

3. How do you identify the spirit of pride?

_____
_____
_____
_____
_____
_____

4. How do you relate to this passage?

_____
_____
_____
_____
_____
_____
_____

5. What in the passage applies to you?

_____
_____
_____
_____
_____
_____
_____

6. What does the Bible say about pride? Is pride a sin?

_____
_____
_____
_____
_____
_____
_____

7. How willing are you to allow your husband to be the head while you submit to his authority?

_____
_____
_____
_____
_____
_____

8. How does your ego affect the relationship between you and your husband?

_____
_____
_____
_____
_____
_____

9. In marriage, "I" is replaced by_____.

_____
_____
_____
_____
_____
_____

10. What will you experience when self-centeredness, pride, and ego is absent from your life?

_____
_____
_____
_____
_____
_____
_____

11. Write your prayer pertaining to the subject at hand.

_____
_____
_____
_____
_____
_____
_____
_____
_____
_____
_____
_____
_____
_____

# Help-Meet

*And the LORD God said, It is not good that the man should be alone;*
*I will make him an help meet for him.*
*Genesis 2:18 KJV*

Many women have misunderstood the term, "help-meet." Many see it as an offensive term, believing it translates as maid, servant, or slave. Whether you call it help-meet or helpmate, it is not meant to degrade you. Rather, it means to promote and show off your ingenuity, power of influence, and effectiveness. As your husband's help-meet, you are his assigned companion, meant to complement and propel him into perfection. You are positioned to meet your husband's needs.

A help-meet protects the heart of her husband, and watches his back at all times to ensure he is fulfilling his duties. A help-meet does not conspire with church members or anyone else to crucify or persecute her husband. Therefore, think twice before complaining about your husband's failures, issues, or problems. Your responsibility is to make sure everything goes well with him and that he accomplishes his goals and assignments. Your husband's failure can be a reflection of your failure to carry out God's instruction as a wife on his behalf.

Now that you know your role as a help-meet, I hope you will enjoy serving your husband. Being a help- meet and a virtuous woman allows you to use your various skills and expertise to assist your spouse in reaching his full potential. You can help your husband become better and catapult him into fulfilling his purpose. Although he is labeled "the head of the household," never assume that he has everything taken care of or under control. God saw that your husband, on his own, may allow many important aspects to fall through the cracks. Soon, you will find out that you may have to teach him a few things. God made you his assistant (help-meet) to remind him of the essential duties. As Aaron and Hur held Moses' hands up and brought him to victory (Exodus 17:11-12), so should you hold your husband's hands up and keep them high. You are his eyes, ears, hands, and feet, so to speak.

God blew the breath of life into the man (Adam), but He took His sweet time to create the woman (Eve). Have you ever wondered why? In my opinion, God knew the virtues that were missing in the man, so He made sure they were found in the woman. Women are the driving force behind many outstanding organizations, businesses, and associations in which men are at the forefront receiving all the recognition and promotion. Did you know that most successful men became successful because of their help-meet? It is the unwavering support, the unyielding encouragement, the powerful influence, and the empowering inspiration of their wives that propelled them to pursue their dreams. My sister, you are not just valuable, you are powerful, influential, and indispensable.

Due to your husband's ego, you may not realize that he depends on you for decision-making, whether in church, home, or business matters. Your husband craves your opinions and ideas. He may not ask you directly for your input, but as his wife and helper, pay close attention to every detail in the home or church. Ask questions diplomatically and offer your assistance.

As the enemy seeks to oppress your mind and distort your focus, he may subtly whisper, "Your husband is the head, yet you are doing all the work." "Look at all you are doing for your husband, home, and church, and it all goes underappreciated." Beloved, Satan will try to discourage you from fulfilling your assignment to your husband. He will paint the picture so well and believable that you react based on what you hear and perceive. Stop! Think! Who calls you? Whose servant are you? Resist his temptation. Cast down and bind every negative whisper. Continue to do what God gave you the strength and grace to execute. Complete your assignment with joy and humility.

Remember, your husband is one of your many ministries. Therefore, do all you can with the spirit of excellence, the right motive, and good intentions. Love him unconditionally as you continue to groom him along the journey. Your efforts will not be in vain; they have the potential to make a significant and positive impact. Be the best help-meet you can be.

# Questionnaire

1. How satisfied are you with your role as a help-meet?

_____
_____
_____
_____
_____
_____
_____

2. Describe what it's like trying to adjust to this way of life.

_____
_____
_____
_____
_____
_____
_____

3. What is your viewpoint on a help-meet?

_____
_____
_____
_____
_____
_____
_____

4. Has your mindset changed since you read this passage? If so, explain.

_____
_____
_____
_____
_____
_____

5. How do you feel stepping in your purpose as a help meet?

_____
_____
_____
_____
_____
_____

6. List ten of your duties as a help-meet.

_____
_____
_____
_____
_____
_____

7. Did this passage bring clarity to anything you had questions about? If so, please share.

___

8. True or False: Being your husband's help-meet gives you permission to usurp authority.

___

9. What are your plans to become a better help-meet?

___

10. What difference would you like to make as a help meet for your husband?

11. Write your prayer pertaining to the subject at hand.

## Married and Lonely

*...As I was with Moses, so I will be with thee:*
*I will not fail thee, nor forsake thee.*
*Joshua 1:5 KJV*

A great number of married women complain about feeling alone and lonely despite living at home with their husbands. Their husband's emotional absence and physical busyness trigger feelings of neglect, abandonment, and sometimes depression.

There are many contributing factors that can cause women to feel lonely, even though married. For instance, army wives whose husbands have been deployed overseas for years are prone to loneliness. Wives of police officers, doctors, and men who work extremely long hours and are exhausted when they arrive home may complain of loneliness. The wives of men who work on ships and are gone for months at a time also fall into this category. Women whose husbands live in another country and may see each other once a year, can experience intense loneliness.

Feelings of loneliness in all these situations are perfectly understandable. But how can a woman's loneliness be explained when her spouse lives in the same house, perhaps sleeps in the same bed, breathes the same air, and touches shoulder to shoulder?

The wife of a deacon explained it this way: "My husband and I are like two strangers sharing the same apartment. He works twelve-hours per day, and when he is home, I feel ignored and neglected, as if I don't exist. He never invites me to go with him anywhere. As the priest of the house, I expect him to make time for devotions and family time; instead, he's either sleeping or watching television. We don't do anything together. Furthermore, he excludes me from all his business affairs and plans."

Many young girls and women dream of marrying their "Prince Charming" with hopes of living "happily ever after." They envision a fairytale wedding with hundreds of guests and strutting around an elegantly decorated ballroom. Some imagine being transported by a horse-drawn carriage, while others may prefer a simple beach wedding with only a few guests. Regardless of the type of wedding she envisions, the bride sets her heart on spending quality time with her husband. Possibly, she has marked her calendar with surprise getaways, date nights, multiple vacations, and so on. Unfortunately, after the wedding and honeymoon have ended, the reality of life sets in, and everything returns back to normal. The great anticipation she felt of being the "virtuous wife of the year" may have been only wishful thinking.

Most couples fully participate in their wedding preparations. They are preoccupied with planning the venue, dress, food, cake, and entertainment. On their wedding day, they make an extra effort to ensure that the event goes smoothly.

*Married and Lonely*

Regrettably, after the excitement is over, little to no time is spent planning how to cope with and conquer pitfalls, disagreements, financial deficits, and other dilemmas when they arise in the marriage. Often, couples spend most of their time away from each other, perhaps working at two or three jobs outside the home. In this scenario, they may be too exhausted to engage intimately, which can result in built-up frustration. Unfortunately, they poured more energy and effort into preparing for the symbolic act of marrying than planning for the actual experience of being married.

Thus, couples may skimp on building a firm foundation strong enough to withstand their marital storms. They have no strategy on how to maintain, nurture, and keep the marriage alive, and as a result, they may have allowed communication and respect for each other to break down. When this happens, they may find that they are no longer attracted to each other and that their sexual desire gradually declines. With no accountability or consequences, they may do whatever they feel like doing and behave as if they were still single. The wife feels unappreciated and unloved, while her husband feels ignored and disrespected. Thus, the rift deepens and the blame game ensues, which may cause the marriage to collapse.

Brace yourself. You will inevitably experience challenges and periods of loneliness in your marriage. Life has its ups and downs, and so does married life. During the down days, however, it is important not to feed a hostile atmosphere. Some couples fight their way through the down days and arise victoriously; others may struggle to get out of their marriage rut to keep the marriage intact. Never take it personally or blame yourself when your spouse shuts down, goes silent, or refuses intimacy. They may be grappling with their own demons and inner struggles and reluctant to share these or seek help, fearing that no one will understand but will judge them instead.

**The Kingdom Woman**

If you are married to an evangelist, missionary, apostle, pastor, or teacher, be prepared for your husband being away from home several times per month throughout the year. Depending on the anointing and calling of his life, he may be invited to preach, teach, or speak in another city, state, or country. One might expect you, as his wife, to accompany him on every assignment, which may not be feasible. Sadly, he may be traveling alone on most of his trips, which may cause you to feel blanketed with feelings of loneliness.

As unbelievable as it may seem, even if your husband is home seven days per week, twenty-four hours per day, you may *still feel lonely*. 'How is this possible?', you may ask. Although he is home, he may spend excessive time in his study either preparing messages, researching, or counseling others. Being the wife of a leader or someone whose attention or service is in high demand can be a lonely life indeed. If you find yourself struggling with feelings of loneliness, you may ask yourself the following questions:

- *How can I cope with and conquer loneliness?*
- *How can I cope with going home to an empty bed at night?*
- *How can I cope with waking up to the echo of my own voice, staring at blank walls, and dining alone?*
- *How can I cope with not having my priest available to share devotions, humor, and laughter?*
- *How can I cope when my husband is a room away, but I can't see or speak with him?*

- *How can I cope with being in the company of hundreds of people and still feeling alone and lonely?*

These are all legitimate questions. However, you do not cope with your own strengths. You can and will cope—not with your own might or power but through the Holy Spirit and the grace of God. It would be an exciting moment for Satan and his agents to see you walk away from your marriage and ministry with bitterness seething through you. I am not making light of your loneliness and desire for your husband's company. However, while your flesh is starving for affection and attention, please think about the advantages and disadvantages of the situation.

You may be thinking that this isn't what you signed up for or thought it would be. I agree. Nevertheless, do not allow loneliness to consume you. Although difficult, try to focus less on your physical needs and the missing components; instead, gaze at the bigger picture. Discern the intent of God and how valuable those alone moments are to your spiritual growth and purpose. Hold Mathew 6:33 close to your heart. Delve deeply into that verse and ask God to reveal its hidden treasure. I encourage you to view your situation from a positive standpoint.

During your time alone, seize the opportunity to work on your own goals, dreams, and visions. Allow your heart and spirit to rejoice for your husband, knowing that he is fulfilling his commission to feed and win souls for the Kingdom of God. Continuously intercede for him. The physical absence of your husband gives you the opportunity to spend more uninterrupted time alone with God. Quality time spent with God equals spiritual growth and a fortified spiritual foundation. Being alone with God should trigger continuous self-examination, attitude adjustments, and the desire to be a better wife.

The more time you spend with God, the more your focus should shift to His attributes, intent, and purpose for your life, ministry, and marriage. Your physical or emotional needs will not disappear, but you will be better able to cope without anger and animosity weighing you down. God is faithful and covenant-keeping. Even if everyone walks away from you, He is with you. In your darkest night, staring at blank walls, He is with you. My sister, God is with you during the deafening silence. He is watching over you as you are crouched down helplessly in the corner of your room. Feel His gentle hand wiping away the tears as they trickle down your beautiful face.

Amid the deafening silence, listen to the sweet, still voice saying, *"My child, you are more than a conqueror. You have overcome many things, and this will be no different because I, the greater one, lives inside you. I will never leave you nor forsake you. I will keep you in perfect peace if your mind stays upon me. Come, let us reason together. You are chosen, you are peculiar, and you are not your own. You belong to me; I redeemed you in Jacob and glorified you in Israel. Fear not. Be not dismayed, for I am your God; I will help you and hold you with my right hand of righteousness."* Beloved, God is not a man that He should lie; neither is He the Son of man that He should repent (Numbers 23:19). God will fulfill His promises to you. WAIT on Him.

Even when we ignore God and place idols and other people above Him, He is still there, watching over and protecting us. Your disappointment, discouragement, and thoughts of quitting the marriage may flood your mind. You may wonder why God didn't show you this part of the journey before, but how would you know your strengths and weaknesses if He had? How would you learn to depend on and trust Him to be there for you? God's love for you exceeds that of your husband, parents, and everyone else. Again, consider these lonely days as an opportunity and privilege to spend meaningful time in the presence of God. Allow Him to groom and build a godly character in you. Subsequently, you and your gifts will develop spiritually as you become a better wife to your husband. Continue seeking God. You will experience His glory, love, faithfulness, and protective power in your life.

**Let us explore some of the reasons why married people can be lonely.**

**Unpreparedness**

First and foremost, many people were <u>NOT READY</u> for marriage, love, commitment, or accountability when they affirmed, "I do." The affection and tolerance for each other were missing; the red flags were flying at their highest but were ignored. Some people proceed with the ceremony not because they love each other, but out of fear of what the invited guests, family, and friends would say if they backed out.

**Disappointment**

Many married couples are disappointed with themselves and each other because their spouses turned out to be the opposite of who they thought they were when they met. Some perceive that the effortless way marriage is portrayed on television is reality, so they make no attempt to preserve and fortify their marriage. Then, when things begin to fall apart, they realize that they had unrealistic expectations of their marriage. They now feel that they have nothing in common and, therefore, no compatibility.

**Financial dilemma**

Often, financial issues can cause couples to be at odds with each other and perhaps even live in torment and fear. One spouse may squander money and create unnecessary debt, causing the family to experience a financial deficit. The other spouse may be a stingy miser who refuses to spend money or take care of the necessary financial obligations to keep the family comfortable. The consequence of such conflicting behavior and the lack of honest communication about money may cause home foreclosure, vehicle repossession, and termination from employment. When *trust, love,* and *respect* are breached, the real family problems begin.

**Infidelity and immorality**

Lust causes many couples to engage in extra-marital affairs, believing that life will be better than that at home. When their infidelity is exposed, they can become belligerent and behave in a hostile and aggressive manner. Disrespectfully, they use strong negative words to describe one another. Feelings of betrayal and emotional disconnect naturally follow, as does loneliness.

**Poor communication**

Like two ships passing in the night on a dark ocean, so are some couples. They continuously pass each other in the house but barely speak. Some couples become secretive and tip toe around when they are conducting business, starting a project, or doing something significant. They no longer seek each other's opinions, express their emotions, or voice their concerns about the state of their marriage. Yet, they often expect each other to know what they are thinking or doing.

Some couples tend to dance around tedious subjects, avoid having sensitive conversations, and become defensive when a particular topic is mentioned. When they do speak, they can appear to be talking to a brick wall. Many blame the other for the lack of communication in the home, insisting that they are always misunderstood or ignored.

**No time spent together**

As mentioned before, some couples spend extensive time away from each other, working at two or three jobs to meet their basic needs. Others may be chasing wealth, fame, or acceptance in other individual pursuits. Before they know, they are becoming estranged from each other and slowly drifting apart emotionally. Sooner or later, they separate, perhaps with divorce in mind.

**Unmet emotional needs**

Companionship is one of the many aspects of marriage that couples look forward to. However, the reality can be highly disappointing. When a partner does not receive affection and attention, or feels they are not being listened to and validated, it can trigger feelings of abandonment, rejection, and inadequacy. As a result, the affected partner may shut down and eventually isolate.

**Incompatibility**

During their courting, couples tend to believe they have found their soul mate because it seems they are emotionally, physically, and spiritually connected. They share the same goals, feel connected emotionally, and don't hesitate to express their needs and concerns. They understand each other perfectly and show great interest in each other's values.

Their views about life, children, finances, careers, and religion are the same. They bond over shared activities, with affection beaming from their eyes, and express unlimited support for each other. Unfortunately, after the marriage ceremony and a few months of living together, the mask begins to peel off, and lo and behold, they find they have nothing in common. Feelings of being deceived, frustration, disappointment, and resentment set in. In the end, this all leads to loneliness.

**Same-sex attraction**

Many people who are married to the opposite sex struggle with strong feelings for the same sex. They may not have physically engaged with a same-sex person, yet this conflict creates a tug of war in their spirits. Because they know homosexuality is not right, they are constantly fighting their feelings and their same-sex attraction has become a fixation that appears to be unshakable. This preoccupation and struggle affect their compassion, love, and desire for their partner, and they may drift away in solitude, leaving their spouse feeling slighted and deserted.

**Busyness**

Busyness is a thief of time, a destroyer of relationships, and an obstacle to a productive life. Both spouses are guilty of allowing busyness to interfere with their marriage. A wife may be married to her job, household, children, social media, and friends to the extent that they consume her entire day. Similarly, a husband may spend most of his time working on his business, attending meetings, alone in his study, and enjoying leisure activities with friends. The couple's time is spent on everything and everyone else except each other. Being too busy to acknowledge the need for intimacy and the longing to be in each other's company may leave a void–a feeling of emptiness. Before long, loneliness knocks at their hearts' door.

**Witchcraft/spiritual warfare**

The late Pastor Layton Smith once shared his story of an encounter on an airline flight coming back from the mission field. Sitting next to him was a stunningly beautiful lady with whom he anxiously wanted to speak but didn't know how. After the meal was served, he realized that the young lady was not eating.

"You're not hungry?" Pastor Smith asked.

"No, I'm fasting," she responded.

"Oh, great! Which church do you attend?" Asked Pastor Smith.

"I don't go to church; I am a witch, and we are fasting to break up marriages worldwide." She said.

Reader, don't be ignorant of satan's devices or tactics. He has assigned agents to carry out his wicked, evil plans against your health, marriages, finances, and destiny. Possibly, many broken marriages and dislike for each other could result from satan's cohorts coming together for its destruction. Spiritual warfare is real. Don't turn a blind eye to strange occurrences in your marriage or home.

To some readers, this may sound farfetched, weird, unbelievable, or nonsensical. However, to many, it is an *"aha moment"* when the light suddenly comes on. To others, the Bible scriptures about spiritual warfare come alive. Some may say, "Finally, someone is willing to shed light on spiritual wickedness and the work of darkness against the innocent."

Witchcraft can affect your marriage and life in many ways. For example, some individuals enter marriage without knowing their spouse's beliefs, practices, or spiritual backgrounds. There are people who knowingly and unknowingly make covenants with the devil for various reasons, hence, giving permission to demons to be a part of their lives. Possibly, the repercussions of such actions can be that, these demonic spirits later became their spirit husband or wife.

Because of the covenant, they are forbidden from engaging in real marriage. If they break the covenant and marry a normal person, the demonic spirits become enraged and begin to torment them. There can be significant consequences of this, such as miscarriages, constant arguing for no apparent reason, and a sudden dislike and possibly hate for the other, which, at its worst, can lead to divorce, or even murder.

If an unaware spouse who is not a part of the covenant allows the demonic spirits to engage them in sexual intercourse, although everything may appear to be okay, it is far from it. Have you heard about incubus (male) and succubus (female) spirits? These are demonic spirits that have sex with individuals while they are asleep. So, when you dream of having sex with your spouse, an ex-lover, or someone you know, it's not just an ordinary dream. These are also known as *familiar spirits*. They take on the form of someone with whom you are familiar so you feel comfortable in the act. The moment of engaging in the sexual act, the evil spirit that enters your body may manifest in various forms of illness, unexplained pain, or a rift in the relationship.

How many times have you heard a person say the following: "I'm treated like a king or queen, but I don't understand why I don't love him or her the way I used to." "I can't stand the sight of him or her. His or her presence and voice irritate me to the point of anger." Many unexplainable divorces, sudden dislikes for each other, or lack of sexual desire for one's spouse can be the result of evil interference. Please do not underestimate the spirit world; it is as authentic as you are reading this book.

Beloved, it may be the manifestation of rulers of darkness, principalities, and spiritual wickedness in high places. As God opened the eyes of Elisha's servants to see into the spiritual realm (2 Kings 6:17 KJV), may He open yours. Do some research on spiritual warfare; it is real. Pray without ceasing; cover your marriage and yourself with the blood of Jesus.

*For the weapons of our warfare are not carnal, but mighty through God to the pulling down of strong holds; casting down imaginations, and every high thing that exalteth itself against the knowledge of God, and bringing into captivity every thought to the obedience of Christ.*
**2 Corinthians 10:4-5 KJV**

*For we wrestle not against flesh and blood, but against principalities, against powers, against the rulers of the darkness of this world, against spiritual wickedness in high places.*
**Ephesians 6:12 KJV**

**Where do you go for assistance if you are married and lonely?**

Begin with your spouse. Choosing the right time, place, and topic to discuss with your significant other is imperative. Avoid saying, "We need to talk," or "I need to talk to you." Those words coming from a wife can feel threatening to her husband. He may start thinking of ways to defend himself. Instead, use comments such as, "Honey, I would like to share something with you; when is the best time?" or "Babe, I have an idea. I would like you to tell me what you think of it." or "Dear, do you have a minute? I would like to show you something." If trying to solve the issue on your own doesn't work, try talking to one of the following people:

*Your pastor or bishop about counseling for both of you:*

- *A Biblical/Christian counselor*
- *A clinical psychologist*
- *A trusted and mature confidante*

Beloved, be intentional about spending quality time with each other and engage in meaningful discussion. Work intensely to create a loving, long-lasting marriage. Set aside some time each week to check in with each other. Understanding where your partner is mentally, emotionally, financially, spiritually, and physically is crucial. Make sure you allow the Holy Spirit to be the CEO, director, and supervisor of your life. With Him in those positions, coming together with your spouse to communicate about various aspects of your life and the awesomeness of God will be exciting.

*"In the mighty name of Jesus, I cover your marriage with the powerful, uncontaminated blood of Jesus Christ. May God bless and keep your marriage. Be honest with each other, exercise trust, show respect, and express love for one another. Say goodbye to loneliness."*

# Questionnaire

1. With a sincere commitment to being truthful who would you honestly say caused the shutdown or rift in your marriage?

_____
_____
_____
_____
_____
_____
_____

2. How is loneliness affecting your marriage?

_____
_____
_____
_____
_____
_____
_____

3. What was your reaction when you discovered that you spent more time alone than with your husband?

_____
_____
_____
_____
_____
_____
_____

4. What are your regrets being married?

_____
_____
_____
_____
_____
_____

5. What have you vented to God about concerning your loneliness?

_____
_____
_____
_____
_____
_____

6. How does the feeling of loneliness affect your relationship with God?

_____
_____
_____
_____
_____
_____
_____
_____
_____
_____
_____

7. Express your heart's desire to both God and your husband. What would you say to them?

_____
_____
_____
_____
_____

8. Explain why you feel lonely or isolated, even in the company of others.

_____
_____
_____
_____
_____
_____
_____

9. Can you be yourself around your husband? If not, why?

_____
_____
_____
_____
_____
_____
_____
_____

10. How is your emotional support?

_____
_____
_____
_____
_____
_____

11. How do you plan to address the topic of loneliness with husband?

_____
_____
_____
_____
_____
_____

12. Knowing what you know now, what would you have done differently?

_____
_____
_____
_____
_____
_____
_____
_____
_____
_____

13. Who have you reached out to during your lonely days? Who do you vent to?

_____
_____
_____
_____
_____
_____

14. Can you recall when the disconnection between you and your spouse began? What was the trigger?

_____
_____
_____
_____
_____
_____

15. Do you rush to judgment and assume the worst when your spouse becomes quiet? What are you thinking, and why?

_____
_____
_____
_____
_____
_____

16. Do you feel more content when your spouse is not home? If so, why?

_____
_____
_____
_____
_____

17. Do you feel sad and experience panic attacks when you know your spouse is close to coming home? If so, explain why.

_____
_____
_____
_____
_____

18. Have you shared the times when you feel depressed or stressed with your spouse? If so, what was his response, and how does it make you feel?

_____
_____
_____
_____
_____

19. Have you ever felt like being somewhere other than home? Does that desire make you physically present but emotionally absent in your marriage? If so, how do you plan to remedy this?

_____
_____
_____
_____
_____
_____
_____
_____
_____
_____
_____

20. Are you experiencing unexplained anger toward anyone? Why?

_____
_____
_____
_____
_____
_____
_____
_____

21. Write your prayer pertaining to the subject at hand.

## Chapter 3

# The Marriage

*By wisdom a house is built, and by understanding it is established; by knowledge the rooms are filled with all precious and pleasant riches.*
*Proverbs 24:3-4 ESV*

*I*t is important to understand that there is a battle against God-ordained marriages. The enemy is waging a war on humanity, seeking to distort and destroy God's blueprint for marriage. But in the midst of this, let us not forget the beauty that a godly marriage brings. It is a union built on respect, communication, love, faithfulness, loyalty, dedication, selflessness, patience, compassion, longsuffering, understanding, wisdom, and humility. A marriage is a partnership of two, yet it is also a unified one, connecting us to a larger purpose.

*For this cause shall a man leave his father and mother, and shall be joined unto his wife, and they two shall be one flesh.*
Ephesians 5:31 KJV

Most young girls and women dream of marrying their "Prince Charming" with hopes of living "happily ever after." Many have envisioned a fairytale wedding with hundreds of guests strutting into an elegantly decorated ballroom. Some imagine being transported by a horse-drawn carriage, while others request a simple yet intimate beach wedding with only a few guests. Regardless of the type of wedding envisioned, the bride sets her heart on spending quality time with her husband. Possibly, she pre-fills her calendar with surprise getaways, date nights, multiple vacations, and much more. However, it is equally important to understand that after the wedding and honeymoon, the reality of life settles in and everything returns to normal. This post-wedding reality is just as significant as the wedding day itself, and being prepared for it is essential to a successful marriage.

Most couples fully participate in the wedding preparation, preoccupied with the entertainment of guests and the perfection of the venue, dress, food, and cake. On the anticipated day, they make an extra effort to ensure the event goes flawlessly. Regrettably, after the excitement around the wedding is over, little to no time is spent on planning how to cope with and conquer pitfalls, disagreements, financial deficits, and dilemmas when they arise in the marriage. Both spouses may spend most of their time away from each other, sometimes working two or three jobs outside the home, and then being too exhausted to engage intimately, which results in built-up frustration. Obviously, more energy and effort were poured into the *present* than the *future*.

Marriage is a ministry, and it should not be entered into casually. It takes two like-minded people to produce a successful marriage. God created man to be the head of his wife and household, but the wife keeps the head aligned. By honoring the king in your husband, your marriage can weather any storm. Marriage is a joyous, yet delicate journey; it brings immense happiness and fulfillment but must be cherished, protected, maintained, and handled with care.

It is incredible how individuals spend quality time planning and arranging every tiny detail of their wedding but barely put any thought or emphasis on survival strategies for their marriage. By investing time and effort in preparing for marriage, couples can empower themselves to navigate the challenges they will inevitably face and enjoy the journey together. With proper preparation, there would be little to no divorce.

Disappointingly, many individuals enter into marriage blindly, unprepared, and unequipped, with preconceived notions and often a prenuptial agreement reflecting the attitude that "What is mine remains mine; what is yours is ours. If I do not like you tomorrow, we can file for divorce." Marriage must not be entered into for selfish reasons. In your marital relationship, **make your spouse your best friend**, confidante, and companion. It is God's perfect will for men and women to settle down, join in holy matrimony, and cherish each other. **If you lose your friendship with each other, sooner than later you may lose the marriage.** Hebrews 13:4 KJV states, *Marriage is honourable in all, and the bed undefiled....* God deems marriage as sacred.

The reality of marriage sets in after the excitement and celebration of the wedding has waned.

You will soon discover that marriage is not always a bed of roses and that it also comes with thorns and briers. Marriage is a lifetime commitment that demands hard work, consistency, dedication, and discipline. It requires respecting each other's opinions, ideas, and dreams while caring about the well-being of your spouse. It also demands exercising patience, a virtue that can bring calm and reassurance in times of difficulty.

Like women, men can be moody too. Therefore, you must be strategic in identifying the right time to engage your husband in a conversation. It is imperative that you make an effort to have in-depth conversations about the marriage, each other, the children (if any), the future, finances, and life in general. Lack of communication can eventually cause spouses to lose interest in each other and the relationship, and then love can turn into hate. Promise God, yourself, and your marriage that you will not carry old, unnecessary baggage from past hurts and trauma into your marriage relationship. If you haven't yet released the pain inflicted upon you by others, please do so quickly; if not, you may ruin a beautiful relationship. Importantly, never allow your friends, coworkers, family, or even strangers to know more about you and what's going on with you than your spouse. Finally, do not expect what you are not willing to give.

# Questionnaire

1. How much do you value and support your husband's dreams, opinions, and ideas?

_____
_____
_____
_____
_____
_____
_____

2. What does this marriage mean to you?

_____
_____
_____
_____
_____
_____
_____

3. How do you plan to get through tough times?

_____
_____
_____
_____
_____
_____
_____

4. Do you have any regrets concerning your marriage? If so, explain.

_____
_____
_____
_____
_____
_____

5. What are your struggles in the marriage?

_____
_____
_____
_____
_____
_____

6. List the prerequisites of marriage. Which one is missing from your life?

_____
_____
_____
_____
_____
_____
_____
_____
_____
_____

7. What is your long term goal for your marriage?

_____
_____
_____
_____
_____
_____
_____

8. How do you honor the king in your husband?

_____
_____
_____
_____
_____
_____
_____

9. Express your heart's desire concerning your marriage and relationship with God.

_____
_____
_____
_____
_____
_____
_____

10. Have you ever considered divorce? Why?

___

11. How did you reconcile your marriage?

___

12. Knowing what you know now, what would you have done differently?

___

13. What is your advice to those who want to or already have their plan in motion to get married?

_____
_____
_____
_____
_____
_____
_____

14. How are you cherishing and protecting your marriage?

_____
_____
_____
_____
_____
_____
_____

15. How solid is your marriage and your friendship with your spouse?

_____
_____
_____
_____
_____
_____
_____

16. List a few reasons why a marriage can become undone.

17. Would you fight for your marriage? Why or why not?

18. What have you identified that can cause a rift in your marriage? How will you fix it?

19. How do you plan to prevent small issues from becoming gigantic problems?

_____
_____
_____
_____
_____
_____

20. On a scale of 1–10, how do you rate your marriage?

_____
_____

21. Write your prayer pertaining to the subject at hand.

_____
_____
_____
_____
_____
_____
_____
_____
_____
_____

## Ten Misses That Can Cause a Rift or Divorce

So many things can contribute to divorce or a rift in marriages. Below are ten possible reasons that can cause strain in a marriage and lead to separation or divorce.

### 1. Misunderstanding

- Understanding is a key factor in maintaining a healthy relationship. Often, spouses find themselves in conflict due to a lack of understanding, leading to unnecessary friction.

### 2. Misleading

- A wife may deliberately deceive her husband into believing that she can get pregnant when in fact, she knows that she did a tubal ligation (tying or cutting of the fallopian tubes).

### 3. Misconstruing

- Some spouses may understand what is said but deliberately misinterpret it, sometimes to soothe themselves or provoke the other spouse.

### 4. Miscommunication

- Clear communication is crucial in any relationship. When couples fail to express their needs or intentions clearly, it often leads to misunderstandings and the blame game.

## 5. Misinformation

- The husband eagerly awaits valuable external information before making a life-altering decision, and the wife takes the phone message but conveys the wrong information, costing him dearly.

## 6. Misjudging

- Judge not lest he be judged, according to the Word of God. One of the worst things spouses can do to each other is to jump to an unfair conclusion and form an opinion about something that is untrue.

## 7. Misconception

- There is a huge misconception that when one gets married, everything will be okay—that there will be no hiccups or misunderstandings. However, when couples begin living together, they soon realize that they were misinformed and that the reality was misconceived.

## 8. Misfortune

- Despite the vow, "For better or worse, till death do we part," when unforeseen illness or trouble arrives, the healthy spouse neglects and abandons their partner. Without hesitation or second thought, they leave the marriage.

## 9. Mistakes

People make honest mistakes that can be overlooked, but some can be costly and deadly. For instance, a couple is about to lose their home to foreclosure. They were encouraged by a family member to do a quitclaim deed. One party agrees and the other says they should hold onto the house a little longer. Before long, they lost the house.

## 10. Miscarriage

- Marriage is a journey of growth and resilience. Numerous times, out of frustration and disappointment, husbands walk away from their marriage because each time their wives get pregnant, they miscarry. However, just as a seed must break open to grow, one can also miscarry one's assignment, purpose, and destiny, only to emerge stronger and more determined.

My hope is that you will never have to face or deal with any of the above. But if you do, seek God's direction and instruction first, before you think about separating or divorce.

## Communication

*Come now, and let us reason together, saith the Lord: though your sins be as scarlet, they shall be as white as snow; though they be red like crimson, they shall be as wool.*
*Isaiah 1:18 KJV*

Texting and sending messages via email or social media platforms are not the kind of communication required for building or maintaining a strong marriage. It is impossible for any relationship to thrive by technological communication only, yet alone marriage. It is so sad that no one talks to each other anymore, people are increasingly estranged from each other, love has grown cold, and compassion and empathy toward humanity are lacking. I have seen individuals show more love and care for their dogs than they do to humans. It can seem as if your existence does not matter anymore—not to your children, spouse, siblings, or other family members.

Technology has destroyed many relationships and marriages, which wasn't God's intention when he created the woman to accompany the man. Communication is one of God's greatest attributes. He values

His children's communication with Him and with each other. It is extremely important to understand that communication is a two-way street between God and His children. He told us in Isaiah 65:24 KJV (paraphrased) *that it shall come to pass, that before we call, He will answer; and while we are still speaking, He will hear. God told Moses, And there I will meet with thee, and I will commune with thee from above the mercy seat, from between the two cherubims which are upon the ark of the testimony, of all things which I will give thee in commandment unto the children of Israel* (Exodus 25:22 KJV). If we are made in the image of God, we are expected to do what He does. God is a communicator; He speaks, He doesn't text.

Due to a lack of communication, many marriages have suffered devastating breakups brought on by tiny issues. Because they are so small, couples believe they are insignificant. When left unattended, however, a small hole in a gigantic ship will eventually sink it over time. Broken-down communication can lead to resentment, malice, bitterness, and even hatred. For example, although it is not uttered, one partner believes the other should know why they are upset and keeps silent. Conversely, the other partner thinks, "If you do not want to talk, I do not have to talk to you." Now, an irreparable rift is slowly causing the marriage to fall apart. Before you know it, one or the other is filing for divorce stating irreconcilable differences.

The quality of communication is highly significant in successful marriages; it is often considered the master key to a good relationship. While I agree it is essential, I firmly believe that *respect* is the *true master key* to a solid relationship. Without respect, effective communication becomes impossible. It is impossible to truly listen to the other when there is no mutual respect. Communication is a complex process that involves more than just talking. It also includes nonverbal cues, which can be just as important in understanding your partner. If the significance of communication after marriage is not established during courtship, it is not uncommon for a spouse to become more introverted after the wedding. By recognizing the importance of communication early on, you can make an informed decision about your partner's suitability for a lifelong commitment.

Continuous communication is the key to unlocking compatibility. Meaningful conversations allow you to gauge whether you share the same areas of brokenness, lack, or pain, and conversely, whether you are compatible after you become successful and there's no more lack. You are in the driver's seat, with the power to assess and understand your relationship dynamics.

During the introductory phase of a relationship, you will learn more about your spouse. His anticipation of being with you is a powerful motivator for him to open up and be vulnerable. His best self is on display during this period, as he is a good listener, offers great advice, and shares from his heart without holding back. Communication seems effortless in this phase when there is no commitment, and the focus is on the excitement of getting to know each other.

However, assumptions can lead to misunderstandings and breakdowns in your relationship. When you start *assuming*, it means you have stopped communicating. Avoid assuming that your husband knows what you need or want to say. You must clearly communicate your needs and desires and make sure he understands what you are saying. Most women believe their husbands are mind readers and body language interpreters who will automatically know their heart's desires. However, this can lead to frequent misunderstandings when communication is broken down.

Be intentional. Prioritize your relationship by setting aside dedicated time for heart-to-heart talks with your husband. Choose a location away from home and distractions, such as his church office if he is a pastor, to create a sense of solemnity. To ensure you cover all the important topics, write down what needs to be addressed. This is a time for transparency, for openly communicating your likes and dislikes, needs and wants, and verbalize your feelings, frustrations, disappointments, and discouragements.

Bear in mind that he may not say what you are expecting to hear. You may not see eye to eye on many issues, and he may not understand most of your concerns. Resist the temptation to hold it against him and to express disgust or contempt. Remember, you are his counselor, a role that involves providing guidance and support. You may have to indirectly ease into a teaching mode. Use this moment to share with him about women's needs and desires. That is an excellent way to get his attention and participation. Enlighten him on what you would like to talk about and gain during your conversations. **Show** him what you are saying and ask what he doesn't understand. Taking notes during conversations is crucial.

Even after fifty years of marriage, there will always be more to learn about each other. This ongoing discovery is a beautiful part of your journey together. It is imperative for couples to prioritize and set aside time to share their opinions and ideas on how to navigate the present and prepare for the future. Your thoughts and feelings are an essential part of the relationship. Find ways to keep the communication fresh and engaging. Communication is the lifeline of your marital relationship; therefore, don't hesitate to use it fruitfully. Do not wait for your marriage to hit rock bottom before seeking help. Some issues can be addressed by reading self-help books, while others require immediate action. Discuss strategies to improve your relationship before problems escalate.

At this point, seeking a kingdom counselor or psychologist is highly recommended. Yes, I know you are praying and fasting for God to fix the situation, and that is great. However, continue to pray and ask God to direct you to the right counselor who He has equipped with knowledge to encourage, enlighten, and uplift His people. Ask Him to direct you to one who abides by and instills godly principles for healthy marriages. Out of pride, fear, or feelings of discomfort, your husband may reject the idea of counseling. Nonetheless, do not give up. Push forward; find a counselor who does not know you or your husband. Choose one who is not a male chauvinist or a narcissist, but who will listen attentively without casting blame, ranting about themselves, or showing bias. I wish you a long-lasting, joyous friendship and an unshakeable marriage.

# Questionnaire

1. Do you believe you always know what your husband wants without him verbalizing it?

___

2. What happens when a spouse stops communicating?

___

3. What caused the communication breakdown in your marriage?

___

*Communication*

4. What was the communication like during your courtship?

_____
_____
_____
_____
_____
_____
_____

5. Where do you see your marriage heading due to lack of communication?

_____
_____
_____
_____
_____
_____
_____

6. List some reasons that can cause a marriage to deteriorate slowly and painfully.

_____
_____
_____
_____
_____
_____
_____

7. How can stubbornness and disobedience manifest devastatingly in a marriage? Please explain.

_____
_____
_____
_____
_____
_____

8. In what area does your husband fail to provide for you?

_____
_____
_____
_____
_____

9. What makes you afraid to communicate with your husband about certain matters?

_____
_____
_____
_____
_____
_____
_____

10. How often do you jump to a conclusion about a matter and later discover that you were wrong?

11. True or False: Assumptions can lead to misunderstandings and breakdowns in your relationship.

12. How important is communication to you and your marriage?

13. On a scale of 1–10, how would you rate the communication in your marriage? Elaborate.

_____
_____
_____
_____
_____
_____

14. Express your heart's desire concerning your marriage relationship.

_____
_____
_____
_____
_____
_____

15. What have you swept under the rug and refused to talk about with your husband?

_____
_____
_____
_____
_____
_____

*Communication*

16. Why do you avoid talking about certain topics?

_____
_____
_____
_____
_____
_____
_____

17. How is keeping silent about certain issues affecting your marriage?

_____
_____
_____
_____
_____
_____
_____

18. Complete the following: Good communication skill can…

_____
_____
_____
_____
_____
_____
_____

19. Learning about each other is never-ending; therefore, what should you focus on now? The past, present, or future? Why did you choose that answer? Explain.

___

20. Write your prayer pertaining to the subject at hand.

___

## Respect His Role as a Husband

*Nevertheless let every one of you in particular so love his wife even as himself; and the wife see that she reverence her husband.*
*Ephesians 5:33 KJV*

As a man of God, your husband may have a spiritual discernment that you haven't yet grasped. His role as your guardian is to keep you safe, as your protector to provide security, and as your provider to continuously attend to your material needs. Trust in his wisdom and guidance, and you will find that the honor and respect you show your husband will make him more responsive to your needs. Respect in marriage is a two-way street, a shared journey rooted in love, commitment, and obedience. It is a biblical principle for wives to reverence their husbands. So, when you are tempted to disrespect the leader of your household, remember the command of your heavenly Father. This principle is not just a cultural norm but a divine instruction to guide both of you in your marriage.

Respect is a *significant* factor for men. Men always desire respect, especially in the home and more so from their wives. If your love for your husband diminishes, he may not even notice as long as he is shown respect. Respect to a man is what love and communication are to a woman. In addition, the way you strongly desire your husband's undivided attention is the same way he desires your respect and honor. Remember, respect is not one-sided. It is a mutual exchange that strengthens the bond between you and your husband, promoting a healthier relationship. You may think he doesn't deserve it, but don't allow that to deter you from your wifely duties. Who determines what one deserves?

As a kingdom wife, showing respect shouldn't be defined by his actions. Never allow your husband to feel like a stranger, an outcast, or an underdog in his own home. Help him iron out his wrinkles, be the wife God called you to be and leave the rest to God. It has been established that your husband is the head of the wife, as Christ is the head of the church. God placed him in this leadership position for a reason. Irrespective of his flaws and shortcomings, view him as someone of great value. Do not get distracted by his weaknesses; instead, celebrate his strengths. It is imperative that you understand the importance of respecting your husband. Lack of respect for your husband reveals lack of respect for God.

Should your husband ask you to disconnect the relationship between you and "sister Sue" because of her constant gossiping and tale-bearing, do not find a hundred reasons to prove that she is a good person and should remain in your life. As a protector and a watchman over your soul, he is protecting your ear gate, soul, and spirit man from continuously entertaining sin. If he states that he is uncomfortable with you attending the weekend retreat with your girlfriends, be humble about it and stay home. Avoid incubating thoughts of him trying to control you or dictate your life. Instead, focus on the positive aspects of his care and concern for your well-being.(Please read Romans 8:28.)

*Respect His Role as a Husband*

It is important to avoid negative expressions in your relationship. For instance, refrain from saying, "You are always gone. You are never home to help me with anything. I have to do everything around the house and struggle with the kids, home, and schoolwork alone." Instead, find ways to support his efforts. Remember, he is making *sacrifices* for you *and* the children. If he doesn't work, you would have no house to care for while the children cry, "Mommy, we are hungry." Express your appreciation to him for being a hardworking, supportive husband. Acknowledge his role as a provider, as there is nothing more rewarding to a man than his wife acknowledging his hard work and expressing her gratitude.

If you are the sole provider working outside the home while your husband stays home, it would be fair if he shares the responsibilities of the household chores and helps with the children. While sharing household duties may come naturally to some men, it's essential to communicate with your husband about the assistance you need. Avoid giving him the impression that you can do it all and that he is not needed. This fosters a sense of partnership and mutual respect in marriage.

As a married woman, you can no longer behave as if you are still single or too independent to seek your husband's advice or assistance. Get rid of the "I am in control; I do not need a man" mentality. Your husband wants to know that he is needed. He wants to feel needed. Refrain from executing projects or doing things yourself as if he does not exist or his input does not matter. Your husband would appreciate being informed about your agendas or any new ventures you are embarking upon. Pursuing a career or starting a business or any other undertaking without including him or asking his opinion can crush his manhood/ego. Undoubtedly, there will be an unsettled feeling of being kept in the dark, disrespected, and treated like a housemate instead of a soul mate. Let your husband feel like a man.

As one flesh and out of respect for his priestly role, share your plans with your husband as you would with your friends or family members. Bring your plans to his attention and consider asking questions such as the following:

*"Honey, what do you think about me starting this business?"*

*"Dear, is it okay if I join this organization?"*

*"Babe, I have this great idea; I would like you to be a part of it."*

*"Sweetheart, I am thinking about going back to school. Here is the information. The course will last one year, Monday through Thursday, and the tuition is $9,000.00. What do you think?"*

When you involve your husband in your plans, you are not just sharing your life with him; you're building a stronger, more unified relationship. It's a way to show him that you value his role in your life and care about the union. This will make him feel a sense of belonging, respected, and powerful. Remember, it's not just his blessings that you need, but also his financial and emotional support. Denounce pride and do it God's way. Imagine if the roles were reversed, and your husband never asked for your opinion or shared his plans or successes. How would that make you feel? Treat him how you want to be treated.

Being mindful of your tone and actions is crucial, especially during heated moments. Actions such as slamming cabinet doors, hissing through your teeth, rolling your eyes, or sighing in disgust during a conversation or moments of disagreement can be deeply hurtful and damaging to your relationship. Instead of reacting, try to understand your husband's perspective. This is not just a way to show respect, but also a valuable opportunity to learn and grow. Always remember, respect for your husband and God should guide your tone and action, ensuring that it is not condescending. Always strive to resolve differences before going to bed. Isolating yourself in another room is not the solution; it's a step away from unity and displeasing to God.

*Let the husband render unto the wife due benevolence: and likewise also the wife unto the husband. The wife hath not power of her own body, but the husband: and likewise also the husband hath not power of his own body, but the wife.Defraud ye not one the other, except it be with consent for a time, that ye may give yourselves to fasting and prayer; and come together again, that Satan tempt you not for your incontinency.*
1 Corinthians 7:3-5 KJV

# Questionnaire

1. What are your husband's roles? Does he exemplify Christ?

_____
_____
_____
_____
_____
_____

2. On a scale of 1–10, how is your respect toward your husband?

_____
_____
_____
_____
_____
_____

3. How is your husband's level of respect toward you?

_____
_____
_____
_____
_____
_____

4. Can you identify what depleted or encouraged your respect for your husband?

_____
_____
_____
_____
_____
_____
_____

5. If you have lost respect for your husband, how do you plan to restore it?

_____
_____
_____
_____
_____
_____
_____

6. What changes do you see in your husband's actions since your respect for him has lessened?

_____
_____
_____
_____
_____
_____
_____

7. How do you show respect and honor to your husband?

_____
_____
_____
_____
_____
_____

8. Do you believe that your husband is satisfied with the level of respect you have shown him?

_____
_____
_____
_____
_____
_____

9. Can you recall the last time you showed dishonor toward your husband and the reason for it?

_____
_____
_____
_____
_____
_____

*Respect His Role as a Husband*

10. How do you think God feels about you dishonoring His servant (your husband)?

___

11. When are you planning to apologize to your husband for disrespecting him?

___

12. True or False: It is a biblical principle for wives to reverence their husband.

___

13. Which role is your husband not fulfilling? When will you talk to him about it?

_____
_____
_____
_____
_____
_____

14. Write your prayer pertaining to the subject at hand.

_____
_____
_____
_____
_____
_____

## Be an Extraordinary Listener

*My dear brothers and sisters, take note of this: Everyone should be quick to listen, slow to speak and slow to become angry.*
*James 1:19 NIV*

Listening is not just a skill but a shield that protects you physically and spiritually. As a kingdom woman, your spiritual ears must be opened and inclined to hear God's direction and plan. Active listening in the spirit realm can empower you to intercept the enemy's plots and assignments against your marriage, mind, and ministry and provide a powerful defense that prevents spiritual dangers from harming you. Most importantly, it equips you with knowledge and aligns you with God's purpose for your life, giving you a sense of control and confidence.

The lives of many prophets were saved in the olden days because their spiritual ears were tuned to the voice of God. Conversely, many lost their position, possessions, and lives because they refused to listen. The inability to listen to God's voice can hinder your spiritual growth and lead to devastating consequences. On the other hand, intentional listening can effectively protect your purpose, your family, and your destiny. Unfortunately, the importance of listening is often realized too late, maybe after a divorce or separation.

Listed below are some common requests often made by either partner in the marriage.

- *Please don't do that anymore, I do not like it.*
- *I prefer if you do not leave that there.*
- *Please let me know when you take money from the account.*
- *Will you please stop creating unnecessary debt?*
- *If you are not able to pay the bills on time, please let me know ahead of time.*
- *Even if I might get upset, please do not lie to me.*

Regrettably, the partner to whom these requests are directed often overlooks or underestimates them, leading to a lack of change. However, intentional listening can be a transformative force in your marriage. It's not just about using your ears, but also paying attention to your body, heart, and spirit.

Common complaints from husbands include the following: "My wife never listens; she thinks she knows everything. She seems to have the solution before she hears the problem. Moreover, it's irritating when I'm sharing vital information about a particular situation and get interrupted by my wife trying to finish my sentences, without knowing what I'm about to say." This sentiment is shared by many men who find themselves in a similar situation. As a result, most men reserve their opinions and remain quiet.

Whether it's a casual chat or a heated debate, mastering the art of listening is crucial. Listening is a skill that everyone can learn. Many men internalize their feelings not because they want to ignore you, but because they're not sure when it's safe to say what they've been thinking or struggling with. They are afraid of being vulnerable, of being knocked down or ridiculed, or of having the issue thrown back in their face. Therefore, when your husband expresses a desire to talk, it is vital to first disconnect from any potential distractions. This means emotionally and physically distancing yourself from work, social media, children, the phone, or anything else that could interfere. Do not miss the opportunity if he reaches out to share his innermost thoughts. Give him your full attention. Ensure you are facing him, lean in, maintain eye contact, and respond quietly by nodding in agreement. He needs to know that you are fully present and that you care.

Depending on the nature of the conversation, you might say things such as, "Hmm, I see," "Oh wow, interesting," or "I got you," when these responses are appropriate. Do not pretend to understand when you don't. Let it be known that his statement is unclear and ask for clarity. Please allow him to finish his sentences and take notes if necessary. Also, remember that non-verbal cues, such as nodding, maintaining eye contact, and mirroring his body language, can convey understanding and empathy. These cues are just as important as your verbal responses in showing that you are actively listening and trying to understand. One of the many benefits of listening is that you will learn what you did not know.

You are probably not alone in feeling that "not listening" is one of your husband's weaknesses, as many other women feel this way about their husbands. However, like many other men, he seeks reassurance that he has a wife with whom he can confide and trust. He wants his wife to listen attentively without interrupting his train of thought, being judgmental, or interjecting her thoughts or self-centered stories. I guarantee you, if your husband can trust you to listen without any preconceived notions, he will open up to you like a broken dam. A man wants to feel a sense of security, knowing that you will always be there for him. He may simply be needing an outlet to vent. Trade places for a brief moment. Can you recall a time when you desired your husband's listening ear? Can you remember wanting to be heard *without* his input, solutions, or criticism, but instead, you felt ignored and unimportant? Understanding each other's need for communication is extremely important for a harmonious relationship. Patience is key in these moments.

Beloved, here are some words of encouragement for you. When there is an intense disagreement, and your husband is upset to the point of raising his voice, remember the power of your calm tone. Avoid fueling the fire by raising your voice. I understand; you are a grown woman, and no one should be speaking to you that way. Nonetheless, when he raises his voice, you should respond with a low, calm voice to achieve peace. Just as throwing gasoline on a fire does not extinguish it, yelling at each other at the same time does not solve the issue. Listen, find out what caused him to be furious, and try to change or fix it. However, do not listen only because you are waiting for the opportunity to point out his weaknesses and flaws. Do not listen because you want to devalue, humiliate, and prove him wrong, to make a point, or make yourself look better. Keep in mind that you have an unseen guest who is watching and listening to everything that goes on in your home.

# Questionnaire

1. Define "attentive listening."

2. How do you handle miscommunication?

3. If I asked your husband how well you listen, what would he say?

4. Are you a person who jumps to provide answers and solutions before hearing the problem? How do you plan to taper that attitude?

_____
_____
_____
_____
_____
_____
_____

5. List ten traits of attentive listening.

_____
_____
_____
_____
_____
_____
_____

6. Do you often make mistakes carrying out instructions because you are not listening? If so, explain.

_____
_____
_____
_____
_____

7. How important is listening?

8. How well can your husband trust and depend on you to have his back?

9. Think for a moment: Was there a time when your husband was talking about something important to him, but you ignored him and/or took what he said lightly?

# Questionnaire

10. How does not listening affect your marriage and relationship with God?

_____
_____
_____
_____
_____
_____

11. Write out Proverbs 18:13 from KJV and two other translations.

_____
_____
_____
_____
_____
_____
_____
_____
_____
_____
_____
_____
_____
_____
_____
_____

# Forgive Without Compromising

*For if you forgive other people when they sin against you, your heavenly Father will also forgive you. But if you do not forgive others their sins, your Father will not forgive your sins.*
*Matthew 6:14-15 NIV*

The Scripture above is a guiding light that speaks so clearly that even a five-year-old can grasp its profound message. It truly says it all.

Is unforgiveness a sin? Yes, it is. Therefore, when you blatantly refuse to forgive, you have already decided to live in presumptuous sin. Your action says, "God, I know your Word says that you will not forgive my sin if I refuse to forgive those who hurt me, but I do not care. Do what you must. I will take my chances." I may sound harsh here, but it is a truth that calls for introspection and conviction.

*Not everyone that saith unto me, Lord, Lord, shall enter into the kingdom of heaven; but he that doeth the will of my Father which is in heaven. Many will say to me on that day, Lord, Lord, have we not prophesied in thy name, and in thy name have cast out devils, and in thy*

*name done many wonderful works? And then will I profess unto them, I never knew you: depart from me, ye that work iniquity.*
Matthew 7:21-23 KJV

From these verses, we can clearly see that God was not rebuking a non-believer but one who has professed to be a born-again Christian. He was referring to those who continuously dwell in sin without remorse or regard for the consequences. Evidently, it doesn't matter how many repentance prayers you have prayed. It doesn't matter how many demons you've cast out or how often you've fasted. Even though you may have won many souls and helped people get delivered, once you've decided not to forgive your sister, coworker, church brother, or husband, you are in danger of hell-fire unless you make a U-turn and let go of unforgiveness. This is a **weighty consequence that should not be taken lightly**. God will not compromise or go back on His Words. So don't be fooled because He may use you to prophesy, work miracles, or heal the sick. *"You can be fired, and He will still let you work,"* as Bishop Merton Clark stated.

Forgiveness is hard when you are doing it with your *own* strength. Unlimited forgiveness is the principle of Jesus Christ. When He told Peter to forgive seventy times seven, Jesus did not literally mean 490 times. Basically, Jesus was saying that we must forgive the individual(s) as many times as they sincerely repent and seek forgiveness. Forgiveness is not only for the trespasser but for the victim as well. Being able to forgive lifts the spirit of heaviness and removes resentment, affliction, and revenge from *your soul*, spiritually rejuvenating and strengthening you.

You may have heard the story of Nelson Mandela, who was placed in solitary confinement and tortured for twenty-seven years for going against evil. Despite being misused, abused, and humiliated, he said he forgave the perpetrators. Instead of being bitter and resentful, he took a positive stance concerning his incarceration. "I went on a long vacation for twenty-seven years," Mandela said. He chose to view his incarceration this way. His messages promoted the act of forgiveness in the world.

Brandt Jean is the brother of Botham Jean, who was murdered in his own apartment by former police officer Amber Guyger. In October 2019, Brandt addressed Amber in the courtroom, saying, "I forgive you; I love you and want what's best for you. I do not even want you to go to jail; all I want is for you to give your life to Christ. Botham would want the same thing for you, too." Then, the young man asked if it was possible to hug his brother's killer. When the judge granted him permission to hug her, she walked swiftly and fell on his shoulder. With a long, tight grip around his neck, she sobbed uncontrollably with her head still lying on his shoulder. I believe out of disbelief, sorrow, and appreciation, she temporarily loosened her grip, and then hugged him again three times, as she cried aloud: "Oh, what the power of forgiveness can do!"

In Acts chapter 7, the New Testament documents Stephen as the first martyr, who was stoned to death for his faith in Christ. Can you imagine the stones, rocks, and bricks that were striking his skull, face, and body? Yet, he asked God not to hold his killers' sins against them. Jesus requested the same of His Father for those who tortured and killed him. God forbid, if your husband gets involved in situations that cause you to say, "I will never forgive him" or "You don't understand the depth of the pain, hurt, and humiliation he has caused me; I cannot forgive him." Think twice. Whenever your thoughts are negatively harassing you, encouraging you to engage in the opposite of God's teaching, rebuke them. What if you were the one who caused your husband harm and disappointment? What would you expect of him?

I understand that your trust has been broken and that you're disappointed and ashamed. Perhaps at this point, you can't see anything else but retaliation and divorce because the wound is still fresh, and the pain is excruciating. Give yourself time to grieve. Refrain from approaching your husband while you are still angry; it may worsen the situation if you do. Wait for the direction of the Holy Spirit and be prayerful. Spend more quiet time with God until you are calm enough to sit with your husband and discuss the matter.

During your conversation with your husband about the matter, listen keenly without casting blame and refrain from making assumptions, which would make him feel even worse. Listen to his side of the story without becoming enraged. Feel free to express your pain, humiliation, and all your concerns in a respectful way. Moving forward will not be easy, but it will require forgiveness. He must forgive himself, and you must forgive him and let it go. Demand his repentance and apology. Let it be known that you will not accept any excuses in his apology. Choosing to forgive him does not mean you are condoning his actions or that you will tolerate such behavior in the future. You are choosing to let go because it is a requirement for you as a kingdom woman, for your spiritual growth, and to reserve your place in heaven. Your forgiveness will manifest as healing in your relationship, restoring trust and fostering a deeper connection. It will position both of you to receive God's best for your marriage, ministry, and other areas of your lives.

Being a kingdom woman does not exempt you from challenges or troublesome times. The problems you face are real. The fights and your desire to throw in the towel are real. There is no immunity, lifeline, or "get out of jail free" card for you because you are a kingdom wife or the wife of a bishop, doctor, apostle, pastor, or reverend. For you, the temptations are even more significant. While your husband is working on himself, it is crucial that you prioritize your emotional health. Never follow or give into your feelings, as they cannot be trusted. Remember, the flesh is always warring against the spirit. When you sincerely forgive him, you will resist the temptation to throw his mistakes back in his face during moments of disagreement. Give him the chance to earn your trust again as he consistently works on changing old habits. Your cross may be heavy to bear; therefore, leave the situation in the hands of God.

*Cast thy burden upon the Lord, and he shall sustain thee: he shall never suffer the righteous to be moved.*
Psalm 55:22 KJV

*For all have sinned, and come short of the glory of God*
Romans 3:23 KJV

# Questionnaire

1. What is your first thought about this chapter? What grabs your attention?
_____
_____
_____
_____
_____
_____

2. What do you understand about unforgiveness?
_____
_____
_____
_____
_____
_____

3. How hard is it for you to forgive? What makes it hard?
_____
_____
_____
_____
_____
_____

4. Can you recall hurting someone and begging for their forgiveness, but you didn't get it? How did it make you feel? Why were you seeking forgiveness?

_____
_____
_____
_____
_____
_____
_____

5. Define "forgive," "forgiveness," and "forgiven."

_____
_____
_____
_____
_____
_____
_____

6. Based on this chapter and the Word of God, who did you need to forgive but refused to do so?

_____
_____
_____
_____
_____
_____

7. According to Proverbs 21:1KJV, complete this thought: "The heart of my husband is…"

_____
_____
_____
_____
_____
_____

8. Complete this sentence: "I choose to forgive my husband because…"

_____
_____
_____
_____
_____
_____

9. Picture your husband standing before you. What would you say to him concerning a troublesome situation?

_____
_____
_____
_____
_____
_____

10. How do you feel when someone continuously reminds you of your past and uses it against you?

_____
_____
_____
_____
_____
_____
_____

11. How is unforgiveness affecting your marriage, life, and your relationships with God and others?

_____
_____
_____
_____
_____
_____
_____

12. Complete this sentence: "I choose healing instead of revenge for my marriage because…"

_____
_____
_____
_____
_____
_____
_____

13. Complete this sentence: "I know most marriages are being attacked by _____ because..."

14. Complete this sentence: "I will fight for my marriage because..."
_____
_____
_____
_____
_____

15. Complete this sentence: "What my husband did is ... But I will..."
_____
_____
_____
_____
_____

16. How much are you hurting from what he did? Have you lost trust in him?
_____
_____
_____
_____
_____

17. What can he do to rebuild and regain your trust?

_____
_____
_____
_____
_____
_____
_____

18. Complete this sentence: "My husband and I are..."

_____
_____
_____
_____
_____
_____
_____

19. Express what change(s) you would like to see in your marriage and husband.

_____
_____
_____
_____
_____
_____
_____

20. On a scale of 1–10, how would you rate your ability to forgive?

_____
_____
_____
_____
_____
_____

21. Share with your husband all that you've written here. Also, write a prayer about forgiveness.

_____
_____
_____
_____
_____
_____
_____
_____
_____
_____
_____
_____
_____
_____
_____
_____
_____

## Be Best Friends

*Ointment and perfume rejoice the heart: so doth the
sweetness of a man's friend by hearty counsel.*
*Proverbs 27:9 KJV*

*Greater love hath no man than this, that a
man lay down his life for his friends.*
*John 15:13 KJV*

Jesus demonstrated the perfect example of what a true friend is and should be. Only an authentic friend would endure humiliation and lay down their life for another, and that's exactly what Jesus did for humanity. He is a friend closer than a brother (Proverbs 18:24). When we reciprocate and become His friend, He says He will not do anything in the earthly realm without first revealing it to His friend. He called us friends. Being a friend of God ensures you know how to maintain a genuine friendship with your spouse.

*He who withholds kindness from a friend
forsakes the fear of the Almighty.*
Job 6:14 ESV

Be intentional about building a well-fortified foundation of friendship to sustain the duration of your marriage. True friends, even best friends, are not immune to disagreements or conflicts. However, they always strive to avoid hurting each other. They do not retaliate with an "eye for an eye, tooth for a tooth" action. If one friend is hurt by the other, the hurt friend would rather bear the pain, walk away, or sit in silence than respond disrespectfully. **This level of respect and loyalty is what truly defines a friendship.**

Being best friends with your husband will help you overlook serious and frivolous offenses. There will be a sense of eagerness to resolve any dispute and return to normal. When the thought of engaging in extramarital affairs or lying to each other crosses your mind, it will be quickly cast out and dismissed. As best friends, there should be no abuse of any kind (verbal, physical, financial, emotional, mental, or spiritual) found among you. Secrets he has shared with you should not be shared with your friends or anyone else, even if the marriage is dissolved. *A friend loveth at all times, and a brother is born for adversity* (Proverbs 17:17 KJV). What does "all times" mean? It means that even when you do not like your husband, you still have to love him. When he makes you angry, when he displeases you, and when you can't tolerate him, you must love him anyway. This is the essence of unconditional love, a love that transcends all circumstances and endures through all trials.

> *Thine own friend, and thy father's friend, forsake not; neither go into thy brother's house in the day of thy calamity: for better is a neighbor that is near than a brother far off.*
> Proverbs 27:10 KJV

One of the greatest benefits of being best friends in a marriage is that the strong foundation of friendship can be a source of strength in troubled times. When you're on the verge of saying something hurtful to your husband, remember the unique bond of friendship you share. Then, the memories of his kindness, patience and love can help you hold your tongue, offering hope and encouragement in difficult moments.

True friends are a rare treasure, and the bond of friendship in marriage is no exception. Strive to cultivate a genuine friendship with your husband, recognizing the unique value it brings to your relationship. In doing so, your marriage will have a lifeline to hold onto in turbulent times. Throughout the friendship, one may be more dedicated and loyal than the other; nevertheless, you should be inseparable, respectful, and have each other's backs.

As your best friend, your husband's thoughts and ideas should be as important and valuable as yours. Mutual respect is the cornerstone of any friendship, and it should be no different in marriage. Friends should never allow each other to feel inferior or insulted, whether in public or private. Courtesy should be extended at all times. Avoid calling him out of his name. Even after fifty years of marriage, he should still be "Honey," "Dear," "Sweetheart," "Babe," or "Darling." Best friends enhance, empower, encourage, and enlighten each other, avoiding unhealthy competition.

Can your husband depend on you in challenging times? In moments of disagreement, it is vital to not use threatening words and statements, such as: "I am leaving. I will not tolerate this anymore. One of these days, you will come home to an empty house." Even if you don't intend to follow through with the threat, those words have been let loose in the atmosphere. Remember, the power of your tongue can either build or destroy. Your words have the power to either strengthen or weaken your relationship. Your continuous threats may be psychologically preparing your husband to live without you.

Perhaps your husband says it's not if, but when will she leave? Not knowing if one day he will come home to an empty house, he may begin preparing his mind for the worst. As the thought of losing you bombards his mind, he may emotionally zone out of the relationship, bracing for your possible absence. Based on that feeling, his trust and commitment may diminish, and he may emotionally distance himself, which can lead to a separation. Eventually, it will take no effort for him to physically leave. If that happens, you cannot get angry or blame him for leaving. You have been setting the stage for this moment *with your words*.

Along life's journey, your feelings may get hurt unintentionally. It's important to avoid responding impulsively. Instead of raising your voice or being forceful in making your point, approach the situation calmly and with grace. Sit down and discuss any issues that may have arisen, clearing the air in a composed manner. Remember, just because your feelings are hurt doesn't justify retaliatory actions. Perhaps your partner was having a rough day and lashed out in frustration, leading to an escalation. My sister, I encourage you to foster a deep friendship with your partner. Be each other's best friend. When you become best friends, you share laughter and sadness, tears and joy, good times and bad, pain and happiness. This friendship will be your first line of defense in sustaining your marriage.

*Above all, keep loving one another earnestly, since love covers a multitude of sins. Show hospitality to one another without grumbling .As each has received a gift, use it to serve one another, as good stewards of God's varied grace:*
1 Peter 4:8-10 ESV

# Questionnaire

1. How strong is your friendship with God?

2. List six Bible verses that speak about friends or friendship.

3. How strong is your friendship with your husband?

4. What does his friendship mean to you?

_____
_____
_____
_____
_____
_____
_____

5. Is the friendship one-sided? Who behaves more like a friend? Elaborate.

_____
_____
_____
_____
_____
_____
_____

6. How does fostering a friendship with each other help your marriage?

_____
_____
_____
_____
_____
_____
_____

7. How does *not being friends* affect the marriage?

8. What traits of a sincere friend do you identify in yourself and your husband?

9. How do you, the church, your husband, and your marriage benefit from the friendship with your spouse?

10. What do you do to avoid conflicts?

___

11. What do you like and admire most about your husband?

___

12. How likely are you to encourage married couples to foster a friendship with each other?

___

13. What is your heart's desire concerning friendship with your spouse?
___
___
___
___
___
___
___

14. True or False: Being best friends with your husband will help you overlook serious offenses, let alone frivolous ones. There will be a sense of eagerness to resolve any dispute and get back to normal.
___
___
___
___
___
___
___

15. How important are his dreams, goals, visions, ideas, and opinions to you?
___
___
___
___
___
___
___

16. What have you done to show him that you care about the friendship and his interests?

_____
_____
_____
_____
_____
_____

17. Can your husband call you a genuine friend? Elaborate

_____
_____
_____
_____
_____
_____

18. List a few benefits of being friends with your husband.

_____
_____
_____
_____
_____
_____

19. Which married couple do you admire whom you would like to model your marriage and friendship after?

_____
_____
_____
_____
_____
_____
_____

20. Does your marriage attract the admiration of others so much that they would like to emulate it?

_____
_____
_____
_____
_____
_____
_____

21. Write your prayer pertaining to the subject at hand.

_____
_____
_____
_____
_____
_____

## Teach Your Husband How to Treat You

*Therefore all things whatsoever ye would that men should do to you, do ye even so to them: for this is the law and the prophets.*
Matthew 7:12 KJV

You hold the power to teach people how to treat you. Some people are generally treated according to their appearance, wisdom, education, accomplishment, status, behavior, and to whom they are connected. Teaching someone how to treat you depends on how you treat yourself and what you allow others to get away with. Destructive behaviors should not be given a second chance to manifest before they are addressed. The next time may be too late. Remember, your self-respect is essential to setting healthy boundaries in your relationships.

Nabal treated David with contempt. Consequently, Nabal's entire household was about to be massacred by David and his men. But when Abigail, Nabal's wife, was made aware of what was about to happen, she used wisdom and humility to save her household from the bloodbath. Abigail ministered and encouraged David to think twice about his calling and assignment from God and not to get his hands dirty with unnecessary bloodshed, which would burden his conscience. David listened and obeyed her. Guess what? Abigail eventually became David's wife. These biblical examples are not just stories but guiding lights that can inspire us to assert ourselves and set boundaries in our relationships. Please read the entire story found in 1 Samuel 25:1-44. Likewise, Esther became the wife of a king because of her appearance, humility, and wisdom. You can read about her story in the second chapter of the Book of Esther.

Teaching your husband how to treat you right doesn't mean demanding lavish gifts, expensive vacations, a considerable sum of money, or unreasonable expectations. However, if he can afford all of the above, why not? In all seriousness, most men grow up hearing and believing that women are weak and beneath them. In their minds, women are not as intelligent or successful. Based on that notion and what they hear and believe, some men act and mistreat their spouses. Sadly, some men relate to their spouses as people who have no value, significance, or worth. Ladies, we may unfortunately be a part of the problem by allowing continuous physical, mental, financial, emotional, and verbal abuse without putting our feet down and saying *no!* No more. If that is the case, you can be a part of the solution today. No one can control another person's actions or behavior; however, you can control what you will tolerate.

While the man is often seen as the head and covering for his wife, it's important to remember that this doesn't imply any form of inferiority. In my view, husband and wife are equal partners, each playing their God-given roles as instructed. *Husbands, love your wives; wives, submit to and respect your husbands.* This is a necessary aspect of a healthy marriage, and it's important to remember that the husband's command to love his wife like Christ loves the church doesn't automatically mean he knows how to treat her. Some lessons are best learned through observation. Have you ever heard the saying, *"actions speak louder than words"*? It is a powerful reminder that you don't need to shout or manipulate to get the treatment you desire. Your actions, attitude, behavior, and self-respect can serve as a guide for your husband, influencing his behavior. By demonstrating how you want and deserve to be treated, *you can effectively communicate your expectations*. He may forget what you tell him, but he won't forget what he sees or how you make him feel through your actions. Therefore, communicate how you would like to be treated.

By all means, show your appreciation for what you like and don't be afraid to say, "No, I don't like this, and it will not be tolerated." Teaching your husband how to treat you is not a one-sided effort. It takes both of you collaborating to make the effort successful. Your involvement and connection in this process are essential.

Below are some tips that you can embrace in appreciating your husband. Do unto him what you would like him to do for you. Hopefully, he will learn and reciprocate. Remember, he will never forget your actions, so it's okay to be the first to begin exercising these actions. When you incorporate these traits in your life daily, you are not just setting an example but also influencing his actions and reactions. You have the power to initiate positive changes in your relationship.

- Be honest in all manner of conversation with your husband.
- Celebrate his strengths and help him work on his weaknesses.
- Set and maintain boundaries.
- Do not try to change him; accept him for who he is and leave the rest to God.
- Don't be afraid to compliment him on jobs well done.
- Show your appreciation for small gestures.
- Check on him throughout the day to make sure he is okay and that his needs are met.

- Being spontaneous can be exciting, but it depends on where that is coming from. Don't wait for the last minute to make requests and then express a negative attitude if they are not fulfilled.
- Place a value on his time and respect it.
- Resist the temptation to yell or treat him like a child.
- Never forget to say *please* and *thank you;* don't take his willingness for granted.
- Respect his masculinity and role as a man.
- Listen without interruption.
- Take care of yourself; put extra effort in your personal hygiene and attire.
- Don't wait for special occasions to buy him gifts.
- I love you" is so loosely used that its significance gets lost. In addition to saying this, *show* your husband through your actions that you sincerely love him.

Whatever you do, make sure it's from your heart and not only because you want him to do something for you.

On the contrary, here are some things that you need to nip in the bud the moment they occur.

- When he calls you derogatory names
- When he yells at you or hits you
- When he ignores you while you are talking to him
- When he spends an excessive amount of time on social media platforms instead of with you
- When he keeps scrolling through his phone while on vacation or during your dinner dates

Do not allow him to exhibit those behaviors twice. With a calm direct tone, state your dissatisfaction the moment he shows that side of him. Address it and shut it down *immediately*. This immediate action empowers you and puts you in control of the situation. After you state what's on your mind, hold no animosity or resentment. Remember, you are friends. Friends challenge friends every so often. When an individual is respected and treated fairly, he or she may think twice about mistreating you. Overall, you should treat others with dignity and respect at all times irrespective of their status, appearance, or occupation.

# Questionnaire

1. Can you identify with anything from this chapter? Explain.

_____
_____
_____
_____
_____
_____

2. How do you relate to this chapter?

_____
_____
_____
_____
_____
_____

3. Have you experienced negative treatment from your husband? If so, how did you handle it?

_____
_____
_____
_____
_____
_____

4. How have you taught your husband to treat you?

_____
_____
_____
_____
_____
_____
_____

5. How can you tell if he is making an effort to do better?

_____
_____
_____
_____
_____
_____
_____

6. Knowing what you know now, what would you have done differently regarding what you've tolerated from the opposite sex in the past?

_____
_____
_____
_____
_____
_____
_____

7. List five ways to teach someone how to treat you.

_____
_____
_____
_____
_____
_____
_____
_____

8. What do you wish you could change about the way you have been treated?

_____
_____
_____
_____
_____
_____
_____
_____

9. How would you describe the way your husband treats you?

_____
_____
_____
_____
_____
_____

10. How satisfied are you with the treatment from your husband?

_____
_____
_____
_____
_____
_____


11. Do you believe he is satisfied with the way you treat him? _____

_____
_____
_____
_____
_____
_____


12. Are you satisfied with the way you treat him?

_____
_____
_____
_____
_____
_____
_____
_____
_____

13. Write your prayer pertaining to the subject at hand.

## Keep the Fire in the Fireplace (Fan the Flames)

*The wife hath not power of her own body, but the husband: and likewise also the husband hath not power of his own body, but the wife.*
1 Corinthians 7:4 KJV

Most things require maintenance to ensure they remain in excellent working condition, and your marriage is no different. God instructed man to be fruitful and multiply, which means having children. Hence, He created the woman not only as a help-meet for the man, but for them to satisfy each other's sexual desires and enjoy the beauty and purity of it under the covenant. God esteems the covenant relationship, and sex is a pure and beautiful expression of God's divine love. It was designed to be shared and explored between covenant keepers. However, because sex has been abused and mistreated over the years, many see it as dirty, nasty, and taboo. Regrettably, it is rarely discussed in the church or in social groups, as many avoid the topic.

As unbelievable as it sounds, when **some** women become born-again Christians, they view sexual intimacy with their husbands as a sin. Taking showers together and modeling in negligees or nude are deemed immoral or dirty and have become things of the past. As a result, they may not know how or blatantly refuse to comfort or satisfy their husband's sexual needs. What do you do to keep the fire burning in your marriage? Imagine being hit by a devastating snowstorm, when traveling by car or foot is impossible. The snow drifts are high, and the temperatures are below freezing. What can be worse? Perhaps not having enough firewood to keep your home fully heated. During the summertime, when the weather is balmy, it is easy to forget to check if the supplies needed for the winter season are in place.

Just as with any other aspect of life, marriages require regular maintenance. There will inevitably be cold moments, so it is crucial not to wait for warmer times before taking action to keep the fire burning. Some couples allow their marriage to die prematurely because they fail to maintain and check their reserve regularly. Neglecting to maintain your marriage continuously throughout the year may result in turmoil, finger-pointing, and blame-throwing. However, by taking a proactive approach and periodically checking the health of your relationship, you can prevent these issues from arising. This is a commitment that both partners need to make to ensure a strong and healthy relationship.

Keeping the passion or fire in your marriage means paying attention to each other's needs and desires. Don't wait for something drastic to happen or take you off guard. When couples are broadsided by the unexpected, their common excuses are "I didn't know" or "I didn't see it coming." Sometimes it's too late. But with open and honest communication, you can avoid these situations. Keeping the fire burning in the relationship is not limited to sex, although it is a vital component of the marital relationship. Effective communication will ensure that both parties' needs and desires are met. It's critically important to frequently check the health and vitality of the marriage. Therefore, periodically check in with your spouse to find out if he's okay, if there's anything you can do to make the marriage better.

What do you have in your reserve to keep your marriage alive and vibrant? Did you stock up on surplus fire-making components? What are these, you may ask. They are the memories you created during your courtship, the long-term goals you set when you were getting to know each other, the jokes and stories you told that made you both laugh hysterically, the quality time you spent on the telephone and in person, the adventurous out-of-town trips, the spontaneous lunch dates, the eclectic conversation about various topics, and the bucket list you made together. If you have done all or any of the above, there is more than enough material in your reserve to keep the fire burning in your marriage.

Therefore, when the cold days come, and the fire in your marriage is dwindling down, reminisce on the happy warm days you have created together. Go to your reservoir of collected memories, retrieve your happiest moments, and laugh about them again. Reflect on your goals for your marriage. It is counterproductive to wait for the fifth or tenth year of your marriage to begin searching for material to start heating things up. All the necessary components needed to make a fire should be in place during courtship and the earlier months or years of your marriage.

I can't say this enough, after the honeymoon phase, when couples get familiar with each other, they tend to take each other for granted and care less about each other's feelings or needs. Little to no effort is made to have meaningful conversations, let alone spend quality time together being intimate. They have lost interest in pursuing adventure or even sharing the same bed. *Pay attention.* The fire is dwindling down, and soon will die. Again, to keep the passion in your friendship and the fire in your marriage alive, you must continue to make the efforts you did before to win his heart, his trust, and his ring. Perhaps it will take a little extra effort to keep his heart yearning after you, the trust between you stable, and the ring on your finger. Are you willing to put in the work? As previously mentioned, sex is not the only thing that keeps the fire burning in a marriage; however, it is a significant component.

**Let's talk about *sex* for a minute**

Experiencing intimacy with your spouse is a beautiful, shared journey. It's a space where you can be completely open with each other without any need for secrecy or hiding. There is no need for him to sneak out of a hotel room or leave your house before dawn to return to his wife. He is yours; you are his to cherish and hold onto forever.

Some individuals find the subject of sex uncomfortable to talk about. Although it's an awkward feeling, one of the biggest mistakes couples make is not discussing sex, whether during courtship or marriage. Once you are sure about your commitment to each other, state clearly what you will and will not do as it relates to intimacy. That way, there will be no surprises, disappointment, or resentment if you refuse to engage in certain activities. Do not assume that your husband should know how to satisfy your sexual needs because he is a man. Unfortunately, there is no manual on how to please your partner sexually, so you may have to verbalize your preferences.

Furthermore, men are different in many ways. Some men brag about being the best at sexually satisfying their spouse. Yet, many do not understand the genetic makeup and desires of their female partners. The most common complaint from women is that their spouse expects them to reach a climax each time they have intercourse. This is not always the case. When she fails to reach climax, he believes that his performance is poor and that she is unsatisfied. This can lead women to feel pressured and to fake orgasm.

## *Why fake an orgasm?*

There are a few reasons for faking an orgasm. Surprisingly, I have spoken to many women who reveal that they never enjoy their husband intimately. Many confess that they have *never* experienced an orgasm but only faked it. For instance, a woman may fake an orgasm to please her husband and spare his feelings of inadequacy if he reaches a climax within a short time. Perhaps she is not in the mood and wants to get it over with, or perhaps she has lost sexual desire for him.

I believe that most men are unaware of their wives' sexually deprived experiences because they fail to be open and have conversations about their sexual desires and comfort zones. I recognize that it may be awkward for you to express to your husband how, when, and where to caress you. However, he needs to know this to ensure a balanced relationship and in fairness to you both. How else will he know what to do or not to do if you refuse to share relevant information about your desires? You can start by initiating a conversation during a relaxed moment, or by sharing an article or video that resonates with your feelings (**NOT PORN MOVIES!**). If you refuse to enlighten him in this area, and he continues **not to** meet your sexual needs, it would be unfair for you to compare his actions to another person. For example, saying things like, "That would never be John Tom." or "If it was Tom Jones, he would have…" Quit comparing and fix it.

Sexual intimacy is *not* all about reaching a climax; therefore, do not be embarrassed if you have not experienced climaxing in that moment. Not reaching that peak of sexual arousal can be a blessing in disguise because it allows you to spend quality time together. If you desire, it allows you to talk all night until you both fall asleep while still embracing each other. Think about it: typically, everything is over when a climax is reached within a few minutes. After that, some people do not want to be touched or hugged, and one partner may roll over, turn their back, and start snoring. Being able to lie with your spouse while embracing and enjoying each other's company will create a remarkable feeling of togetherness. During moments of intimacy, some individuals want to talk, they want hear feedback and certain words, while others prefer to remain calm and quiet. Commit to start communicating your sexual desires and possible discomfort to your husband; find ways to work on that part of your relationship together.

> *Now concerning the things of which you wrote to me: It is good for a man not to touch a woman. Nevertheless, because of sexual immorality, let each man have his own wife, and let each woman have her own husband. Let the husband render to his wife the affection due her, and likewise also the wife to her husband. The wife does not have authority over her own body, but the husband does. And likewise the husband does not have authority over his own body, but the wife does. Do not deprive one another except with consent for a time, that you may give yourselves to fasting and prayer; and come together again so that Satan does not tempt you because of your lack of self-control.*
> 1 Corinthians 7:1-5 NKJV

How do you fan the flames and keep the fire burning in your marriage? Life doesn't stop because you are a kingdom man and kingdom woman. Do not abandon your hobbies. I guarantee that doing things together will tighten the bond between you. You both will be more relaxed, rejuvenated, and better conditioned to serve God's people.

Listed below are some actions you can take or revisit for the purpose of maintaining or rebuilding your marriage. These should rejuvenate your relationship and eliminate boredom.

- First and foremost, include each other in your devotions, prayers, praise, and worship moments (Pray together).
- Do not take each other for granted.
- Be sensitive to any luke warmness that you may be feeling.
- Pay attention; be vigilant to what is missing in your relationship.
- Protect your marriage from termites and toxins *(interference from friends and family)*.
- Repeat your vows and recommit yourselves to each other.
- Spoil your husband with gifts, not only on special occasions.
- Continue to send him lovely messages as you did during courtship.
- Call him on the telephone from another room and pursue him (role play).
- Occasionally, surprise him with his favorite meals.
- Read to each other and study together.
- If your husband is a preacher, tag-team preach at home—it is fun!
- Encourage your husband to take you on lunch and dinner dates.
- Make memories; plan indoor or outdoor picnics for two.
- Take long walks in the park or on the beach, etc.
- Create laughter by telling jokes and stories.
- Play cards or board games.

- Invite him into the kitchen to cook or bake with you.
- What are your husband's favorite sports? Challenge him to a game, if possible.
- Does your husband go to the gym? Join him and find fun things to do with him.
- On his day off, make a one-night hotel reservation for two.
- Continue calling him those sweet names.
- Take showers together.
- Does he like fishing? If so, plan a fishing trip.
- Do not give up on self-care; still attire yourself attractively and grab his attention.

# Questionnaire

1. Are you satisfied with the intimacy in your marriage?

_____
_____
_____
_____
_____
_____

2. Some women complain that their husbands only touch them when they want to have sex. Is that your complaint as well? How does that make you feel? What are you going to do about it?

_____
_____
_____
_____
_____
_____

3. Women also complain that their husbands do not caress them before, during, or after intercourse. Do you have that problem? When will you address it with your husband? What is lacking in the bedroom?

_____
_____
_____
_____
_____
_____

*Keep the Fire in the Fireplace (Fan the Flames)*

4. How important to you is connecting emotionally before intercourse? Do you meet each other's sexual needs?

_____
_____
_____
_____
_____
_____
_____

5. If you could change two things about your romance or intimacy, what would they be? Why?

_____
_____
_____
_____
_____
_____
_____

6. Have you had discussions with your husband about his performance, your needs, or your disappointment? What was his reaction?

_____
_____
_____
_____
_____
_____
_____

7. Have you discussed with your husband how often you prefer to engage in sexual intercourse, your preferred positions, and how long foreplay should be? If not, what are you waiting for?

___

8. List ten ways to keep the passion and fire burning in your marriage.

___

9. What stood out to you from this chapter? What would you like to talk to your husband about?

___

10. What have you learned and plan to apply to your marriage?

11. What is your view of discussing the topic of sex and orgasm with your husband?

12. If you have faked an orgasm, what was the reason?

13. What do you enjoy most about your husband and your marriage?

_____
_____
_____
_____
_____
_____

14. Are you afraid to talk to your husband about sexual issues? If so, why?

_____
_____
_____
_____
_____
_____

15. List some memories that you have created together.

_____
_____
_____
_____
_____
_____
_____
_____
_____

16. How do you show your husband that you are comfortable and satisfied with the level of intimacy you experience in your marriage?

_____
_____
_____
_____
_____
_____
_____

17. On a scale of 1–10, how satisfied are you with the intimacy? Elaborate.

_____
_____
_____
_____
_____
_____

18. How do you maintain your marriage?

_____
_____
_____
_____
_____
_____
_____

19. From the list above, what do you enjoy doing or would like to do with your husband?

_____
_____
_____
_____
_____
_____

20. Do you promise to communicate to your husband about your sexual desires, comfort and discomfort?

_____
_____
_____
_____
_____
_____

21. Write your prayer pertaining to the subject at hand.

_____
_____
_____
_____
_____
_____
_____

## CHAPTER 4

# The Home

*And my people shall dwell in a peaceable habitation, and in sure dwellings, and in quiet resting places.*
Isaiah 32:18 KJV

Not every home is a Christian home. A Christian home is dedicated to the Holy Spirit and appoints God as the head above everything and everyone else. If God is the head of your home, the environment and atmosphere should be free from misery, strife, disrespect, hate, unforgiveness, malice, anger, selfishness, and bitterness. However, I am not saying you will have no arguments or disagreements. However, because you are spirit-filled and have made God the head of your life and home, those negative spirits cannot linger in such an atmosphere.

As a kingdom woman, encourage your family to pray and share fellowship together. A family that worships and enjoys fellowship together will grow spiritually and emotionally. Because of the comfort, harmony, and love at home, whenever your family members are away from home, there should be an eagerness within all to get back to it. Your duty as a wife and a help-meet is to create a comfortable atmosphere for the family—not as a maid, but as a comely woman. You are responsible for inviting the spirit of God to dwell continuously in your home. Thus, there should be abundant signs that the spirit of God abides there.

Be mindful of who you give access to your home. They can shift the peaceful, harmonious atmosphere into chaos. Your home is a sanctuary for your husband and children; not everyone should be invited to enter it. Discern the spirit of each individual who wishes to visit you at home. Irrespective of your setting aside time to intercede for those you know and do not know, feeding the hungry, and clothing the naked, there are times when you will have to shut out the whole world and its troubles. Your home is a place of refuge and safety for your family. It is the place where you dine together, create memories, laugh together, and share life's journey, with its pitfalls and victories. Stamp the blood of Jesus on your home.

Perhaps your home is viewed as a model home by strangers and your extended family. Even though individuals may influence or inveigle you to do the wrong thing, they expect you to live what you preach, and they are watching to see if you will succumb or be loyal to your faith. There are others who expect you to show hospitality to everyone with whom you come into contact. However, not everyone can be comfortably hosted in your home. For example, your home should be *off limits* to your girlfriends who want to hang out, gossip or influence you against submitting to your husband. It is off limits to those who want to run in and out, not wanting to be fed spiritually, and who cannot feed you spiritually.

To prevent retaliation and backlash, let the church building serve its purpose of being the extended home for its members—not your personal space. Your home should be out of bounds to those who simply want to make mischief and create animosity between your home and the church.

*The Home*

Never take the unwanted problems, members, or affairs of the church to your home. If your husband is the pastor, encourage him to make the church house available to those members who need counseling, mentorship, or advice.

## Questionnaire

1. Describe the atmosphere in your home.
_____
_____
_____
_____
_____
_____

2. If you could change one thing about your home, what would it be and why?
_____
_____
_____
_____
_____
_____

3. How comfortable are you, your husband, and children being at home?
_____
_____
_____
_____
_____
_____

4. How do you create a godly atmosphere in your home?

5. On a scale of 1–10, how is your time of fellowship and praying together at home?

6. How do you handle individuals who seek to come to your house uninvited, with no sincere need?

7. What would you like to say or discuss with your husband after reading this passage?

_____
_____
_____
_____
_____
_____
_____

8. How can you tell if your husband is comfortable at home?

_____
_____
_____
_____
_____
_____
_____

9. If your husband shows signs of discomfort, how do you plan to fix it so he can be comfortable?

_____
_____
_____
_____
_____
_____
_____

10. How do you show your husband that you have created a spirit-filled atmosphere for him?

11. What are your likes and dislikes about your home?

12. How often do you call the family to participate in prayer, praise, and worship at home?

13. Write your prayer pertaining to the subject at hand.

## Do Not Overlook Your Children

*Children's children are the crown of old men;*
*and the glory of children are their fathers.*
*Proverbs 17:6 KJV*

Children are extremely important to God. They are gifts from Him and also His reward from the womb. Children must be nurtured and trained to know, honor, and respect God. They should be dedicated to God from an early age. As promised, Hannah gave Samuel to God when he was approximately three years old. As a result, God began using Samuel by age twelve, who later became a prophet, judge, and priest. Jesus' disciples wanted Him to overlook and dismiss the children, but it angered Him and He refused to comply. Paraphrasing Jesus' words, He said, "leave them alone, let them come to me. They are innocent and pure in heart and thoughts." Ponder this, without children, the world would come to a screeching halt. They are the future.

*Lo, children are an heritage of the Lord: and the fruit of the womb is his reward. As arrows are in the hand of a mighty man; So are children of the youth. Happy is the man that hath his quiver full of them: They shall not be ashamed, but they shall speak with the enemies in the gate.* (Psalm 127:3-5).

*And they brought young children to him, that he should touch them: and his disciples rebuked those that brought them. But when Jesus saw it, he was much displeased, and said unto them, Suffer the little children to come unto me, and forbid them not: for of such is the kingdom of God.*

Mark 10:13-14 KJV

As I listened to a pastor's daughter speak about the reasons why the pastor's children left the church, my heart ached. She stated that she felt as if the church took her parents away, leaving her empty and alone. As a result, she rebelled against her parents and the church. She expressed how much she resented her parents for allowing that to happen and how she hated the church for interfering in her life. In addition, her hatred for the church grew even stronger because of the way the members treated her father as a pastor and her mom as the first lady. Feeling deprived and abandoned can cause children to rebel against their parents and the church. "A child is never happy sharing his or her parents," she stated. Heart rending, but true.

Next, a pastor's son spoke for four minutes about the best and worst things about being a pastor's child. He began with a lengthy list of the worst things first. Then, he said, "The only good thing about being a pastor's kid is getting donuts. You can walk into any room at church and just take a donut, and no one would bother you."

Pastors' children are expected to be perfect, walk in holiness, and have certain beliefs. Unable to live up to the expectations of most church members, these children are put down, talked about negatively, and treated like outcasts. They are often ignored and their character assassinated. Do not expect your children to have it altogether, especially if the seed was not sown in them. One or two grains may have fallen here and there, but if you believe that was enough for them to get it together and be sold out for Jesus, you will be disappointed. Perhaps those seeds fell among thorns, fell to the wayside, or landed on stony ground. Even if they fell on good ground, it must be watered by their parents.

Pay attention to your children. Your children face real struggles and life challenges, but they are often afraid to mention them. The pressure on them is intense. Look at what they are *not* showing you and listen to what they are *not* saying. Moms, make your homes a safe haven for your children—a place where they look forward to being without any thoughts of running away.

Dear beloved sister, if you have children, please allow them to be themselves. Let them go through the normal phases of being children. As you are fully aware, it is pressuring for some adults to be themselves among some born-again believers, let alone these young teens. All eyes are on them, waiting for them to slip and make that big mistake. Sadly, their lives are under a microscope, being watched and scrutinized from every angle.

Listed below are some tips on how to make your children feel safe and unafraid to share their struggles with you.

- Be their parents before being their pastor or first lady.
- Don't be so busy with your members' children that you can't hear the inner screams of your own children.

- Your biological family takes priority over your church family.
- Be sensitive to children's needs for acceptance and attention.
- Be aware that your children can feel lonely and isolated even among hundreds of people.
- Minister to your children one-on-one about accepting Christ as their Lord and Savior.
- Teach your children how to love, respect, and fear God, and to keep His commandments.
- Make time to do the fun things that you used to do with your children.
- Encourage your husband to set aside time to make himself available for the children when they need to open up and speak to *Daddy—not pastor*.
- Make time to be their mentor and teach them the ways, attributes, and character of God.
- Please do not allow your children to believe that they are automatically saved and on their way to heaven because they were brought up in the church and dad is a pastor (if dad is a pastor).
- Counsel them against the spirit of depression, suicide, and drug abuse.
- Protect them from church bullies.
- Do not allow church members to raise your children or dictate your children's lives.

- Your children should know how to apply Godly kingdom principles because they were born and raised in a pastor's home.

- Expecting your children to be deeply connected to God is wonderful, but do not disown them or look down on them with disdain because they disappoint you.

# Questionnaire

1. Have you shared with your children the differences between going to church, being a follower of Jesus, and fostering a relationship with God? What are your expectations of your child or children?

_____
_____
_____
_____
_____
_____

2. Have you identified any traits of rebellion or anger in your children? If so, how do you plan to address this?

_____
_____
_____
_____
_____
_____

3. What are your plans to help your children overcome low self-esteem and lack of confidence, if any?

_____
_____
_____
_____
_____
_____

4. Do you believe you spend enough time with your children? If your answer is no, what are you going to do about it?

_____
_____
_____
_____
_____
_____
_____

5. What makes your children open up to others instead of you and their dad when it comes to their problems?

_____
_____
_____
_____
_____
_____
_____

6. On a scale of 1–10, how happy and secure are your children?

_____
_____
_____
_____
_____
_____

7. How do you plan to make your children feel safe and comfortable to speak to you about their struggles?

_____
_____
_____
_____
_____
_____

8. Have you personally ministered to your children and led them to Christ?

_____
_____
_____
_____
_____
_____

9. Did they confess their sins and accept Christ as their Lord and Savior?

_____
_____
_____
_____
_____
_____

10. Based on your children's lifestyle, where will they spend eternity if they die right now?

_____
_____
_____
_____
_____
_____
_____

11. What would be their answer if your children were asked, "Do you feel loved and appreciated?"

_____
_____
_____
_____
_____
_____
_____

12. Did you teach your children how to live a consecrated life?

_____
_____
_____
_____
_____
_____
_____

13. Write your prayer pertaining to the subject at hand.

## An Inviting Atmosphere

*She watches over the affairs of her household
and does not eat the bread of idleness.
Proverbs 31:27 NIV*

Most individuals gravitate to and enjoy an inviting atmosphere. This atmosphere, when cultivated, has a profound impact on relationships. It is not only created at home; it is created wherever you are by the things you do and say. A man yearns to be in the company of his wife when she displays a pleasant countenance, jovial personality, a caring and compassionate attitude, a listening ear, and an understanding heart.

A blissful marriage results from your husband feeling safe, celebrated, and welcomed every time he is in your presence. A satisfied husband is likely to express eagerness and excitement at spending quality time with you. As a wife, your role in creating a welcoming atmosphere in your home is of utmost importance. This is something that your husband, even if he is disorganized and untidy, deeply appreciates. Your appearance and attitude significantly contribute to this inviting atmosphere. Having your hair in place, wearing clean attire, and having a pleasant smile can greatly influence your husband's mood. Your presence can turn your husband's bad day into a better one and a good day into a great one.

A home is considered a safe haven—a place where you look forward to peacefully unwinding after a long day. Make your home warm and inviting not only for your husband but for the Holy Spirit as well. The soothing melodies of gospel music, the wisdom of sermons, and the comfort of bible reading in the house will not only set a serene atmosphere but will also uplift your spirits. You may say, "I have children, and it is challenging to create a pristine, calm atmosphere with them around." Yes, I agree. I suggest you provide a small area in their room or somewhere away from the main areas for them to play quietly with their toys. You can set your home's tone free from undue disturbance while making sure their needs are met.

As the proverb says, "Cleanliness is next to godliness." A neat, pristine environment will make the atmosphere at home so inviting to your husband and visitors that they may not want to leave. In maintaining your home, keep the environment clean, attractive, and warm. This means keeping shoes away from the main entrance and out of sight and removing all unnecessary items off the floors. In addition, never leave your bed unmade, eliminate any lingering foul odors, and declutter. A kitchen sink and countertop free from unwashed dishes and unused kitchen aids is a beautiful sight.

Continuous complaints, nagging, yelling, and emotional breakdowns can seriously affect the atmosphere of your home. These negative emotions can imbue the atmosphere with heaviness rather than harmony. This behavior is the last thing a man wants to see or hear when he gets home. It is crucial to avoid behavior or attitudes that will displease or turn your spouse off. Remember that a part of your godly assignment is to keep him calm, satisfied, and focused.

## Questionnaire

1. How do you make your atmosphere conducive to the Holy Spirit?

_____
_____
_____
_____
_____
_____

2. What would be your husband's response if he was asked to describe the atmosphere at home?

_____
_____
_____
_____
_____
_____

3. If you have children, what are the challenges you encounter while trying to maintain a pristine home?

_____
_____
_____
_____
_____

4. How do you contribute to maintaining the desired home atmosphere?

_____
_____
_____
_____
_____
_____

5. How do you maintain a godly atmosphere?

_____
_____
_____
_____
_____
_____

6. Do you believe your husband is excited to be around you? Why or why not?

_____
_____
_____
_____
_____
_____

*An Inviting Atmosphere*

7. What is your husband's demeanor when he is around you?

8. How do you show your husband that you have created a spirit-filled atmosphere for him?

9. How does your husband contribute to the home atmosphere?

10. How do your children contribute to the home atmosphere?

_____
_____
_____
_____
_____
_____

11. What does your husband complain about? How do you handle his complaints?

_____
_____
_____
_____
_____
_____

12. How do you plan to fix what he's complaining about?

_____
_____
_____
_____
_____
_____

13. Write your prayer pertaining to the subject at hand.

## Take off the Heels

*A time to get, and a time to lose; a time to keep,*
*and a time to cast away.*
*Ecclesiastes 3:6 KJV*

Take a look at the picture on the cover of this book. This lady is trying to walk on a thin rope in high heels while balancing herself with baggage; she is attempting to juggle multiple things at the same time. She may not accomplish what she sets out to do or make it to her destination. But remember, you have the power to be fully prepared, equipped, and comfortable enough to begin or complete your tasks. Anything that prevents you from fulfilling your duties and moving freely, or that has become a hindrance or encumbrance, should be cast aside. You are in control of your readiness and comfort, which empowers you to tackle your responsibilities with confidence.

When you are at home, it is important to remove any impediments that hinder your movement. Take off your heels and relax. Your husband and children need you to be the stabilizer of the home, and this requires you to move around freely without obstacles. As King Solomon wisely said, "there is a time for everything under the sun." There is a time and place for

*Take off the Heels*

your heels, and there is a time and place for your flat, comfortable shoes. While some may choose to maintain a high-maintenance appearance at home, for most people, being at home is a time to be free of anything that slows them down as they prepare to jump in wherever needed.

When your husband feels disheartened or broken, he needs your support. If he's sitting on the floor, take off your heels and sit with him. Show him that you are sensitive to his pain and that you care about what he's going through. If he cries, cry with him. Lie prostrate with him. Your support will be his tower of strength; therefore, show sincere compassion for his brokenness.

Women in heels can appear very intimidating, so taking off your heels can make you more approachable and relatable to your children. It is a physical act that signals to them that you're not too busy or preoccupied to be approached. This can help them feel more at ease and open to sharing their feelings with you. Make sure that all impediments are removed so that you can see clearly and move freely to carry out your assignments. While others depend on you, God counts on you. Remember, you have a significant role in your family and community. This is not just a responsibility, but also a privilege, as it allows you to make a positive impact on those around you and those who you will meet along your journey.

# Questionnaire

1. Can you identify anything that is standing in your way of being the wife and mother you are called to be?

_____
_____
_____
_____
_____
_____

2. Many women crave happiness, security, wealth, etc. What are/were you craving? Why?

_____
_____
_____
_____
_____
_____

3. How do you plan to eliminate these obstacles?

_____
_____
_____
_____
_____
_____

4. What is your take away from this passage?

_____
_____
_____
_____
_____
_____
_____

5. List a few of your roles as your husband's help-meet.

_____
_____
_____
_____
_____
_____
_____

6. When at home, do your husband and children feel comfortable approaching you?

_____
_____
_____
_____
_____
_____
_____

7. What should you do in moments of despair when your husband feels disheartened and broken?

_____
_____
_____
_____
_____
_____

8. What jumped out or resonated with you from this passage?

_____
_____
_____
_____
_____
_____

9. Some women believe that marriage should be 50/50. The husband should show interest and be equally hands-on with the kids and chores around the house. What do you believe and why?

_____
_____
_____
_____
_____
_____

10. Write your prayer pertaining to the subject at hand.

## Submission

*Wives, submit yourselves unto your own husbands,
as unto the Lord.
Ephesians 5:22 KJV*

Submission is a word that most women detest and defy because they believe they are giving up their rights and independence to please a man. Many women also believe that submission is degrading. Woefully, many tongue-speaking, preaching-machine, demon-chasing women refuse to submit to their husbands. Beloved, it is impossible for you to rebel against your husband and submit to God at the same time. When you rebel against your husband, you rebel against God.

Mighty woman of God, hear me clearly, being submissive to your husband is a win for you, for your husband, and for your marriage. Submission opens the door to peace, contentment, love, and harmony in your home. So, whenever you hear the word "submission," think of a life of peace and an unforgettable marriage in the most beautiful way. Remind yourself that your husband is a part of the mission to which God has called you. Therefore, by submitting to your husband, you are submitting to your mission. When you willingly place yourself under the authority of your husband, together you will be able to victoriously take down any giant standing in your way.

However, submitting to your husband's direction or instruction does not mean losing your sense of self, becoming inferior, or being his doormat. It means you are a wise and intelligent woman who sees her husband through the eyes of God. Additionally, you are honoring and obeying God's Word while respecting your husband and his authority. Nothing is taken or will be taken from you; you are just as independent and accomplished as you were before—only more humble and respectful. Submission is closely related to humility; therefore, where submission is absent, watch out! Pride is present. Submission is a source of strength and confidence.

Failing to submit to your husband indicates a misalignment in your relationship with God. Consequently, you are running on "E" (Empty) as it relates to obedience, reverence, honor, and fear of God. "Oh no, I disagree with that. I have a great relationship with God. I am a prayer warrior," you may say. "Let us hear the conclusion of the whole matter: Fear God, and keep his commandments: for this is the whole duty of man" (Ecclesiastes 12:13 KJV). A great relationship with God includes following His direction, keeping His commandments, and obeying His instruction to love, honor, and submit. It is a relationship built on trust and reliance.

When there is a genuine connection with God, submission becomes a source of peace and contentment. Knowing that you are pleasing God, you will be more than happy to serve and please your husband. Furthermore, you will never see submitting to your husband as unfavorable. A godly woman cares about her husband's well-being and seeks to make him look good, physically and spiritually.

# Questionnaire

1. Before you read this book, how did you feel about the word "submission"? How do you feel about it now after reading this chapter?

_____
_____
_____
_____
_____
_____

2. In what areas are you struggling with submission?

_____
_____
_____
_____
_____
_____

3. What was your first thought when you heard the word "submission"?

_____
_____
_____
_____
_____
_____

4. What would your husband's answer be if he was asked about your reaction to submission?

_____
_____
_____
_____
_____
_____
_____

5. Why do you hesitate to submit to your husband?

_____
_____
_____
_____
_____
_____
_____

6. How do you feel knowing that you have readily submitted to strangers but hesitate to submit to your own husband?

_____
_____
_____
_____
_____
_____
_____

7. Explain how pride can prevent someone from submitting to authority.

_____
_____
_____
_____
_____
_____

8. Many followers of Christ fail to submit to entirely Him. How is your submission to God?

_____
_____
_____
_____
_____
_____

9. What does it take to build a relationship with God?

_____
_____
_____
_____
_____
_____
_____
_____

10. Explain why there are so many divorces among churchgoers.
_____
_____
_____
_____
_____
_____
_____

11. Why is it important for a wife to submit to her husband?
_____
_____
_____
_____
_____
_____
_____

12. Why do you believe God says women should submit to their husbands?
_____
_____
_____
_____
_____
_____
_____
_____

13. Should submission be forced or learned? Explain your answer.

_____
_____
_____
_____
_____
_____

14. List those to whom we should submit.

_____
_____
_____
_____
_____
_____

15. Which of the following would be considered submission and will get your point across better? Yelling and slamming of doors, silence because of anger, or a soft tone. Explain the difference.

_____
_____
_____
_____
_____
_____
_____
_____

16. What are your fears about submission?

_____
_____
_____
_____
_____
_____
_____

17. Explain what it means to submit yourself completely to God.

_____
_____
_____
_____
_____
_____
_____

18. How does God feel when you submit your all to Him and not your Husband?

_____
_____
_____
_____
_____
_____
_____

19. Find three Scriptures about submission and write them down and then dissect Proverbs 31.

_____
_____
_____
_____
_____
_____

20. Ponder this: When you are ill, you submit to the instructions of the doctor and pharmacist. At work, you submit to your boss and supervisor. When traveling by airplane, you submit to the pilot and flight attendant. When utilizing public transportation, you submit to the driver. You did not think twice about submitting your life into the hands of people you do not even know. Therefore, what makes it so hard for you to submit to the man you married and promised to spend the rest of your life with? The one you vowed to honor, love, and obey?

_____
_____
_____
_____
_____
_____
_____
_____
_____
_____

21. Write your prayer pertaining to the subject at hand.

## It Is a Thin Line

*Shew me thy ways, O Lord; teach me thy paths.*
*Psalm 25:4 KJV*

"Walking on a thin line" means navigating or striking a balance between two sides, positions, or approaches to something, especially when trying to avoid one of them. There is a thin line between being married and single. There is a thin line between faith and fear, joy and sadness, love and hate, hurting and healing, staying sane and losing your mind. There is an extremely thin line between maintaining your salvation and backsliding, life and death, and good and evil. This line seems to get even thinner as it relates to overseeing the church and your home, along with being the wife of a kingdom man. I am sure you desire to stay on the positive and productive side at all times. However, situations may arise and push you to the side you have avoided.

Remember that giving others easy access to your marriage, home, family, and ministry can be detrimental to your staying on the straight path and maintaining balance. There are those who will provide a safety net for you as you walk across the thin line. Others will guide and cheer you on, encourage you to stay safe, focus, pursue your dreams, and strive for the best. Maintaining focus on positive outcomes is crucial, as this can make you feel hopeful and optimistic about the future. On the contrary, some will maliciously rip away the safety net, place obstacles in your way, and may even cut the line, causing you to lose balance and descend abruptly over the precipice. At the same time, they stand by and watch gleefully.

So many individuals cohabit for years without getting married, and they live their best lives without pressure or worry, it seems. Strangely, after a couple gets married, within six months or less, they are ready to quit the marriage because of what they call "irreconcilable differences," which are often misunderstandings or disagreements that seem impossible to resolve. Perhaps it was a minor disagreement that escalated into a full-blown fight. Hence, it becomes the deciding factor in separation or divorce. Sadly, it appears as if it's better to stay single. The devil is a liar. Can you see the devil's intention here? He seeks to do everything in his power to profane God's plan for marriage so that individuals will continue to live in sin. But remember, the security and joy of a committed marriage far outweighs these challenges.

Be aware of potential pitfalls that can lead you astray, and steer clear of them. Keep Christ at the forefront of your thoughts. Despite the challenges, the critics, the obstacles, or the temptations, remember that with His guidance, you can safely navigate the right path. Fully commit yourself to the personal journey with Jesus Christ. Hold on to His strong and mighty hand, and let Him lead you through life's challenges. With faith, you can overcome any giant, obstacle, or hindrance that shows up along your journey.

# Questionnaire

1. In your own words, define "thin line."

___

2. What are some of the consequences of allowing others easy access to you, your home, and your marriage?

___

3. List a few ways that you can easily fall on the wrong side of the thin line.

___

4. Have you identified anything that can push you over the line? How will you ensure that you stay on the positive side?

_____
_____
_____
_____
_____
_____
_____

5. How do you plan to protect your mind and marriage from falling over the thin line?

_____
_____
_____
_____
_____
_____
_____

6. How will you overcome the giants, obstacles, and hindrances?

_____
_____
_____
_____
_____
_____

7. How do you plan to protect your love from derailing?

_____
_____
_____
_____
_____
_____

8. Have you ever experienced a close call in falling over the thin line? If so, elaborate.

_____
_____
_____
_____
_____
_____

9. What kept you from falling over the thin line?

_____
_____
_____
_____
_____
_____
_____
_____

10. Write a prayer about the subject at hand.

## Balance

*Do not be over righteous, neither be over wise—why destroy yourself?*
*Do not be over wicked, and do not be a fool—why die before your time?*
*It is good to grasp the one and not let go of the other.*
*Whoever fears God will avoid all extremes.*
*Ecclesiastes 7:16-18 NIV*

Most drivers can tell you that they have experienced their car vibrating, drifting off the road, and sometimes drifting into oncoming traffic unintentionally. Repeatedly, they struggle to keep the car in its lane. Could it be under-inflated tires? Is it their steering? Perhaps the brakes are worn unevenly. As they ponder on the various reasons why the vehicle could be vibrating and veering to one side, out of frustration, they seek the advice of their mechanic.

The mechanic's diagnostic test revealed that a wheel alignment and balancing were needed. Obviously, it does not matter whether you have a prestigious, high-end car or a bicycle. Once there is a balance or alignment problem, frustration and discomfort are inevitable. A misaligned or imbalanced vehicle can yield devastating or fatal results. Likewise, if your life lacks balance and proper alignment, it can pose health issues, marital problems, and even mental challenges. As the old saying goes, *too much of one thing is good for nothing.*

Finding balance in all aspects of your life is of the utmost importance. Living a well-balanced life enables you to carry out your responsibilities as a wife, a kingdom woman, and mother *effectively*. Balance is needed in your marriage, home, church, health, secular job, and emotions. *Inconsistency* is a giant enemy and one of the many causes of imbalances many individuals' lives. Failure to be consistent will interfere with the way you balance yourself and your time. Seek to create ways that will bring balance to your home as a wife and mother, and balance in your church as a kingdom woman in a leadership position. If you are the first lady, one way to bring balance to the church is by making sure that all assignments are allocated equally and fairly among church members. *Being the first lady does not mean you assume all the church responsibilities or try to do it all.* I will elaborate further in the upcoming chapters.

It is impossible for you to juggle all the affairs of home, church, and your job, and stay sane. There will be an *overload* on your bodily systems, which may cause your "breaker to chip," so to speak. Everything will be chaotic, in complete darkness, and in disarray. In order to keep your sanity and make others happy, there must be physical, mental, and spiritual balance.

It is amazing how important things can be overlooked and left undone when you're trying to do everything by yourself. While you are busy being a homemaker, your husband and children are starving for your attention and affection. Therefore, identify the areas you need help with at home. Once your children are old enough to do household chores, assign them specific duties. Teaching them responsibility at an early stage in life will be rewarding. Without a bossy tone, respectfully ask your husband to assist you with a few tasks around the house as well.

If you work outside the home and church, never take the caseload or the frustration of your job to your home. Leave work issues at work. Make time for yourself. Meditate, be intentional, and live a purposeful life.

If you are married to a pastor, when you are at church, you are the pastor's wife *first*, your children's mother *second*, and then the first lady of the church. In other words, your husband and family come first, and then the church. Bear in mind that you are there to enhance the church, to be a role model to the members and a tower of strength to your husband. Acknowledge and accept the fact that you cannot do everything in all departments. Your resources, time, energy, and money are limited. However, inconsiderate people will expect you to go above and beyond your call of duty. Do not be afraid to say no when you are asked to perform duties outside your areas of expertise.

With so many people and things vying for your attention as a mother, wife, and first lady, you can easily misplace your priorities. If too much time is given to the church, your home will suffer the consequences, and your husband and children may feel abandoned. Likewise, if too much time is spent with your children and husband, the church feels neglected. Consequently, the murmuring, complaining, resentment, and ill feelings will begin. Strike a balance between being a wife, mother, and the first lady so the church and its duties will not take priority over the needs of your husband or children. Contrastingly, never allow your home life to make you neglect the church, church family, and its duties. As you navigate your way through life, think positively. Indeed, you are walking on a thin line; therefore, balance well.

## Questionnaire

1. List six things that you can do to create balance in your life.

_____
_____
_____
_____
_____
_____

2. What can you do to achieve spiritual wellness and balance?

_____
_____
_____
_____
_____
_____

3. How will you create balance in your church?

_____
_____
_____
_____
_____
_____
_____
_____

4. How do you plan to create balance between home and church?

_____
_____
_____
_____
_____
_____
_____

5. List six areas of your life where balance is always needed.

_____
_____
_____
_____
_____
_____
_____

6. When delegating assignments, how will you prevent burnouts from plaguing the members or those at home?

_____
_____
_____
_____
_____
_____
_____

7. What plans do you have in place for delegating tasks?

_____
_____
_____
_____
_____
_____

8. How do you plan to rise above your current state of imbalance?

_____
_____
_____
_____
_____
_____

9. Complete the following: It is of utmost importance that you find balance in all aspects of your…

_____
_____
_____
_____
_____
_____
_____

10. What are the challenges that come with lack of balance?

_____
_____
_____
_____
_____
_____

11. How can you prevent burnouts in your life?

_____
_____
_____
_____
_____
_____

12. Explain your take away from Ecclesiastes 7:16-18.

_____
_____
_____
_____
_____
_____
_____
_____
_____

13. Elaborate on the word "balance." What does it mean to you?

_____
_____
_____
_____
_____
_____
_____

14. In what areas do you lack balance?

_____
_____
_____
_____
_____
_____
_____

15. Who or what is your first priority? Explain why.

_____
_____
_____
_____
_____
_____
_____

16. Identify and list the areas in your home that need balance.

_____

_____

_____

_____

_____

_____

17. How does lack of balance affect the ministry, church, and marriage?

_____

_____

_____

_____

_____

_____

18. Write your prayer pertaining to the subject at hand.

_____

_____

_____

_____

_____

_____

_____

_____

_____

_____

_____

## The First Lady

*A wife of noble character who can find? She is worth far more than rubies.11 Her husband has full confidence in her and lacks nothing of value.12 She brings him good, not harm, all the days of her life.*
*Proverbs 31:10-12 NIV*

Perhaps the role of being a "first lady" is new to you. It may be unexpected, and you may not have a clue what to do or how to manage your way around the church members and your duties. Maybe it was never your desire to marry a pastor, but your preference was to remain an "ordinary sister." Perhaps his calling to be a pastor came as a surprise, after marriage. Nevertheless, you are a pastor's wife (or soon to be). As the first lady, your private life will *not* be so private anymore; you are now living in a glass house.

I am not sure how and from where the phrase "first lady" derived as it relates to being a pastor's wife. As someone nicely puts it, the term was adopted from secular practice, as if to say, "What is good for the president and the 'first lady' of The White House is good for the pastor and his 'first lady' of God's house." He also implied that since honor and distinction are given to wives of governmental officials or head of states, such as presidents, prime ministers, and governors, the church expects the pastor's wife to be honored because he, too, holds a very important office and is doing a mighty work for God. Regardless of how it came about, I believe it is a privilege and honor to be the first lady of an anointed man of God and a thriving congregation. The first lady's obligation is first to her *husband*, and then to the church.

A pastor stated that he was told, "When the church hires a pastor and placed him on staff, they did not hire his wife. It's a two-for-one deal," Don't worry about not being on staff or being paid. Wherever your husband goes, you go, and as his wife and help-meet, you are assigned by God to assist him along his life's journey, which includes ministry and the church. Within the church, there are many departments in which you can lend your services and expertise. I encourage you to work in the areas in which you are most comfortable and effective and choose the task(s) that you are passionate about. It can be an uncomfortable experience if you assume roles without the necessary knowledge or insert yourself in departments without the experience required. Avoid a life of misery for yourself and those around you by not choosing those roles.

Some pastor's wives become offended because they were not asked or given the opportunity to preach. My sister, hear me well: not all pastors' wives are called to be in the pulpit. Some are called to be the strength behind their husband, or the supervisor of various departments within the church. First, identify your gifts, purpose, and strengths. What do you believe you are called to do? What are your gifts? What do you enjoy doing most? What are your strengths? Are you good at organizing? Are you an excellent event planner? Are you a unique fashion or graphic designer? Are you an efficient administrator?

Whatever you choose to do, you will be watched and scrutinized, and you will sometimes be misjudged and misunderstood. Even though some members may expect you to know and do it all, do not fall for that trap, which will only make you unhappy. If you try to force a puzzle piece where it doesn't fit, it will stand out like a sore thumb. Therefore, do what you can without putting yourself under unnecessary pressure. One of your duties as a first lady is to find out what is needed in the church and to seek assistance from congregants. In some churches, the first lady is hands on. She sets up and breaks down before and after an event. She cleans, cooks, serves, as well as organizes itineraries, bulletins, etc. She tries to fit in and make herself useful in every area. There are some first ladies who will not lift a finger to assist in anyway. Although you are not obligated to take on any tasks or roles, it would be appreciated if you give a helping hand where needed.

Woman of God, be prepared to empower, encourage, uplift, equip, and mentor some of your members, whether through Bible study, Sunday or Sabbath school, biblical counseling sessions, or individual mentoring. The pastor may not be able to handle certain situations and may ask you, the first lady whom he trusts, to intervene. He may also ask you to conduct one-on-one sessions with members who need help resolving personal issues or problems at home. Couples may approach you, seeking advice about their marriage or how to handle their rebellious children.

Please understand that church members may see you, your life, and your marriage as "perfect." Therefore, even when you are bleeding while leading, you're expected to ignore your wounds and bandage theirs without frowning or letting it be known that you, too, are having trouble at home or in your marriage. Never waste an opportunity to win souls for Christ, whether in the church, home, or on the streets. Teach individuals how to build an intimate relationship with Jesus through fasting, praying, and reading the Word. Show them how to examine their lives daily and live godly.

My sister, you will need an outlet to vent to someone or to use as a sounding board. As previously mentioned, you can be in a crowd but still feel lonely in the sense of not having many friends—if any at all. You may not have anyone to talk to and share your troubles with. Loneliness is real. Sometimes, it will appear as if that's all you have. Forming a network with pastors' wives will be extremely helpful. From that network, find at least one person who can be your confidante—someone who will allow you to be yourself without judging you or waiting for you to slip or mess up—someone who will guard everything you confide in them and only take it to God in prayer, not spread it around to the other wives in the group.

Avoid isolating yourself when situations become tedious. Isolation can give place to depression, stress, and feelings of overwhelm. It is impossible for you to tread this journey alone. You may ask, *why do I have to network with other pastors' wives when we have a lot of women in our church?* Yes, there are plenty of women in your church; however, do you know if they are mature enough to handle all that is going on in your life? Can they relate to what you're going through? Are you sure they won't resent you and your husband, or leave the church after you disclose your issues to them? It is best to keep your personal life away from the members. One may act or seem to be mature *until they hear your story.*

Another way to vent is through journaling. Also, praying and reading your Bible and other biblically-based books will keep your mind on God and in perfect peace.

*A disclaimer: As previously mentioned, I am not a pastor's wife and have never been. From a Transformational Life Coach and one kingdom woman to another, this study guide is meant to encourage, enlighten, and uplift you as you navigate through life's pathway.*

# Questionnaire

1. How happy are you with your role as first lady?

_____
_____
_____
_____
_____
_____

2. What do you regret about being a first lady? (if anything)

_____
_____
_____
_____
_____
_____

3. Have you ever dreamed of becoming a first lady? Elaborate.

_____
_____
_____
_____
_____
_____
_____
_____

4. Describe your role as a first lady.

_____
_____
_____
_____
_____
_____
_____

5. As the first lady, what are your expectations from the church and pastor?

_____
_____
_____
_____
_____
_____
_____

6. Where do you see yourself five years from now?

_____
_____
_____
_____
_____
_____
_____

7. What are your plans for the women in the church?

_____
_____
_____
_____
_____
_____

8. What are your plans for the church as a whole?

_____
_____
_____
_____
_____
_____

9. What may cause depression, stress, and feelings of overwhelm? What are your strengths?

_____
_____
_____
_____
_____
_____
_____
_____
_____

10. What are your gifts? How can you use those gifts to enhance and empower the body of Christ?

_____
_____
_____
_____
_____
_____
_____

11. When your husband is transferred from a church, what would you like to be said about you as a first lady?

_____
_____
_____
_____
_____
_____
_____

12. How would you handle being misunderstood, judged, or physically hit by a member?

_____
_____
_____
_____
_____
_____
_____

13. How would you react to a lie that was taken to the church headquarters about you or your husband?

_____
_____
_____
_____
_____
_____

14. What may be the result of isolating yourself when situations become tedious?

_____
_____
_____
_____
_____
_____

15. With whom have you discussed personal matters about your pastor and husband? How do they view or think him now?

_____
_____
_____
_____
_____
_____
_____

16. Write your prayer pertaining to the subject at hand.

## Respect His Office as Pastor

*And we beseech you, brethren, to know them which labour among you,*
*and are over you in the Lord, and admonish you;*
*and to esteem them very highly in love for their work's sake.*
*And be at peace among yourselves.*
*1 Thessalonians 5:12-13 KJV*

Miriam suffered leprosy because she spoke ill of her brother, Moses. Bears ate the children who mocked and jeered Elisha saying, "Go up, thou bald head; go up, thou bald head" (2 Kings 2:24 KJV). Do you remember how wicked Saul was? He attempted to kill David every chance he had. Conversely, David had multiple opportunities to kill Saul and yet he spared his life. God told David not to lay hands on His anointed, Saul. Out of obedience to the instruction of God, David refused to kill Saul even when he had multiple opportunities. Regardless of what Saul did, David would not avenge him or allow anyone to lay hands on him. After Saul's death, David killed the Amalekites who killed him because he, Saul, was God's anointed. Please understand the principle of God's Word. Touch not the Lord's anointed and do His pastors no harm.

I have mentioned this before but it is worth repeating. Irrespective of you being his wife, be extremely careful what you say or do against your husband. Even if he messed up, avoid speaking ill of him. Leave him and the situation to God. The Lord will not hold you guiltless if you lay as much as a straw in His servant's way, causing him to stumble. You will be judged severely if you frustrate or cause pain to His servant. Many individuals have suffered gravely because they criticized and hurt the servants of God.

Although he is your husband, God expects you to respect his office as pastor and your under shepherd. Resist the temptation to speak over the pastor or try to override his decisions or order he has put in place. If a member complains to you about the pastor, listen attentively. Do not defend him, and do not scold or reprimand him in front of the individual or the church. Ask the member, "Do you mind if I take notes of what you are telling me? Would you like me to speak to the pastor about this matter? Are you willing to have a meeting with us, if one is called?"

When there is a disagreement at home with your husband, there should not be any form of resentment or disagreement against his role as the pastor. If you are unable to get over the matter, get in your prayer closet before you leave the house for church and bind up every foul, contrary spirit. Bind the spirit of resentment, offense, unforgiveness, and discord. Strip them from their assignment and render them powerless. Although you are the first lady, you are still a member of the church; therefore, you are expected to listen, obey, respect, and follow the pastor's direction without frowning or making negative remarks.

Out of great respect and honor for the man of God's well-being and safety, position yourself to prepare and fix his water, coffee or tea, and meals at all times. You are there to watch his back and to make sure no harm comes near him. Also, if you believe that your pastor's preached sermon was too surface and non-effective because he didn't expound on the text enough or mispronounced a few words, restrain yourself from drawing negative attention to his weaknesses or his shortcomings as a pastor. Do not undermine his leadership, and do not join other members in belittling your under shepherd.

# Questionnaire

1. What came upon Miriam's body and why? (Numbers 12:1-15)

2. What happened to the children who mocked Elisha?

3. How is your husband's performance as a pastor?

4. How often have you negatively discussed your husband's/pastor's weaknesses and shortcomings with your friends, family, or fellow church members?

_____
_____
_____
_____
_____
_____
_____

5. On a scale of 1–10, how much do you respect your husband's role as a pastor?

_____
_____
_____
_____
_____
_____
_____

6. What has he done that caused you to lose respect for him as a pastor or husband? (if he did)

_____
_____
_____
_____
_____
_____
_____

7. Would you point out to your pastor his errors and shortcomings in love?

_____
_____
_____
_____
_____
_____
_____

8. How do you handle a disagreement at home with your husband versus your pastor?

_____
_____
_____
_____
_____
_____
_____

9. How will taking side with one individual over the other manifest in their behavior?

_____
_____
_____
_____
_____
_____
_____

10. Explain your feelings toward your pastor.

_____
_____
_____
_____
_____
_____

11. Have you been tempted to compete with your husband for the pulpit?

_____
_____
_____
_____
_____
_____

12. Do you find it hard to listen, respect, and obey your pastor? Why?

_____
_____
_____
_____
_____
_____
_____
_____
_____

13. Why is it crucial for you to prepare the man of God water, tea, or food?

_____
_____
_____
_____
_____
_____

14. Write your prayer pertaining to the subject at hand.

_____
_____
_____
_____
_____
_____
_____
_____
_____
_____
_____
_____
_____
_____
_____
_____

## Support His Ministry/Ministries

*Who can find a virtuous woman? for her price is far above rubies.
The heart of her husband doth safely trust in her, so that he
shall have no need of spoil. She will do him good
and not evil all the days of her life.
Proverbs 31:10-12 KJV*

"You finished preaching more than an hour ago, and you are still standing here chatting with Dick, Tom, and Harry. Don't you know I need to go home? Maybe *they* don't have a life, but I do. Furthermore, I have to go to work tomorrow. *Let's go!*" demanded the pastor's wife bitterly.

I cannot emphasize this enough: You are your husband's help-meet—not his *hurt meet*, as one person puts it. He needs your help and support in every area of his life. Being supportive of his ministry is extremely important. You are the gem the Lord placed in his life to make him shine, to enhance his endeavors, and to allow his inner greatness to radiate outwardly. *Supporting your husband's ministries means assisting his visions from conception to birth.*

## Support His Ministry/Ministries

As his wife, you can help ensure that he fulfills his purpose and destiny. You can call forth the hidden treasure and greatness from within him. Your words can encourage him to become the best person God called him to be. However, your words and actions can also contribute to his becoming ineffective and unproductive. Your words are powerful; choose and use them wisely. Be his loyal partner in the ministry. Honor him with your conversation and conduct.

When you aspire to be a faithful partner to your man, you are bringing honor and glory to the name of the Lord Jesus. You are assisting him to become the world's most coveted husband. Conflict may cause you not to see eye-to-eye sometimes; however, it does not negate the fact that you are still expected to perform your wifely or first lady duties. Another way to support his ministry is to identify his need for a break or a sabbatical and encourage him to do so. God's business requires the spirit of excellence at all times. You may be disappointed with his actions and poor choices; nonetheless, you are his business and life partner, and the work of God must continue.

Don't forget that you were placed in his life to help him overcome his hurdles and correct his mistakes. Look beyond his errors and inadequacies as you continue to cover and intercede for him, especially on days when he is not physically or emotionally well. God expects you to show up amid the conflict and support your husband regardless. Your genuine support can change the trajectory of your lives and marriage.

The congregants may not see or know what's going on at home, and by right, they do not need to know. Most church members are not mature enough to handle certain situations, which may cause their relationship with God to be shaken. As a result, some may walk away from the church.

# Questionnaire

1. Describe how supportive you are of your husband's ministries.

_____
_____
_____
_____
_____
_____

2. In what areas could you be more supportive?

_____
_____
_____
_____
_____
_____

3. How do you view his visions?

_____
_____
_____
_____
_____
_____
_____

4. What are your plans to enhance his visions?

_____
_____
_____
_____
_____
_____

5. How often do you speak life, death, or failure in your husband's life, destiny, and potential?

_____
_____
_____
_____
_____
_____

6. Reflect on your thoughts and words toward your husband. Are they empowering and uplifting, or the opposite?

_____
_____
_____
_____
_____
_____

7. From the previous question, how do you empower and uplift your husband?

_____
_____
_____
_____
_____
_____

8. What can you do differently to be a better supporter of your husband's ministry?

_____
_____
_____
_____
_____
_____

9. From paragraph three, complete the following : As a wife I can:

_____
_____
_____
_____
_____
_____
_____
_____
_____

10. How can your genuine support change the trajectory of your life and marriage?

_____
_____
_____
_____
_____
_____
_____

11. What is the consequence for assassinating your husbands' character with friends and family because of his mistakes and short-comings?

_____
_____
_____
_____
_____
_____
_____

12. Write your prayer pertaining to the subject at hand.

_____
_____
_____
_____
_____
_____
_____

# The Church Face

*Beloved, think it not strange concerning the fiery trial which is to try you, as though some strange thing happened unto you: but rejoice, inasmuch as ye are partakers of Christ's sufferings; that, when his glory shall be revealed, ye may be glad also with exceeding joy.*
1 Peter 4:12-13 KJV

*For I know the thoughts that I think toward you, saith the LORD, thoughts of peace, and not of evil, to give you an expected end. Then shall ye call upon me, and ye shall go and pray unto me, and I will hearken unto you. And ye shall seek me, and find me, when ye shall search for me with all your heart.*
Jeremiah 29:11-13 KJV

The "Church Face" is the fake smile and radiant look we often put on to mask our true emotions. This facade can make it appear that all is well and that there are no problems in our lives. Understanding this concept is the first step to addressing it.

There are many reasons why you may choose to wear a church face. Perhaps you dislike a particular group of members or are dissatisfied with the church duties assigned to you. Maybe you're unhappy with the

## The Church Face

responsibilities of being a pastor's wife or a leader. You may also wear a church face because you regret associating with this particular body of believers and their church's regulations.

A few years ago, I met a stunningly beautiful lady named Paula at a church conference. Apart from her attractiveness, something strange about her arrested my attention. After the conference's first session ended, we were all directed to the lower level of the sanctuary, where lunch was being served. I was privileged to be seated among eight friendly women. Pastors, evangelists, missionaries, psalmists, and pastors' wives were sitting at the table, as was Paula. During the conversation, nothing was off limits; the ladies bared their souls to each other, and there was not a dry eye at the table.

"I do not believe any of you have experienced anything to compare with what I have gone through and am still going through," Paula uttered. As the tears streamed down her lovely face, she shared the pain, torment, and hostility she endures at the hands of her husband, who is a pastor. Spellbound, we watched her trembling hands move slowly toward her face. She took off what had first caught my attention about her appearance—a pair of extremely dark sunglasses. She wore them all day indoors during the conference. We all gasped for breath, which was followed by deafening silence. The massive discoloration around her eyes and the swelling of her face stood out against her fair complexion. Our hearts sank, realizing the stark contrast between her public persona and the private suffering she endures.

Paula broke the silence and said, "I am tired of answering questions about my face; that's why I wear sunglasses. I have been telling folks that I fell and hit my face on the doorknob, but honestly, my husband and I had a fight, and my face became his punching bag. I attempted to leave him numerous times, but matters got worse when he found out," she continued. "You guys do not know; he is an angry soul. I am afraid of him. I really love him, and I know he loves me, too, but I believe this is the breaking point," Paula said with a quaking voice, her emotional turmoil palpable.

She also shared that one morning while getting ready for church, some silly thing got him angry, and he began to yell, hit her, and call her derogatory names. In the car, they argued the entire way to church. "As soon as I got out of the car, upon approaching the church door, I put on a big smile and what I call my "church face," pretending that everything was perfect between us. Even before he mounted the pulpit to preach, he gave me the evil, nasty eye," Paula said. "Beneath the surface of my smile are layers of physical, spiritual, and emotional pain, scars, and discomfort, but I have learned to wear it so well."

First ladies, I hope you will never experience this dilemma. Even though you may also wear your "church face" on occasion, hopefully it's not due to your experiencing the above circumstances. Beloved, whenever discrepancies arise in your marriage, I pray that you and your husband find ways to resolve it before the Sabbath or Sunday morning. It is your responsibility to ensure that you present a united front. You can pretend to men that all is well, but the omniscient, omnipresent God sees the realm of the heart. He knows all the hidden secrets.

Avoid wearing the "church face" to cover up wicked acts or to make anyone feel comfortable with their bad behavior. Instead of tolerating abuse and living under false pretenses, you should deal with the matter immediately. I encourage you to seek counseling or ask a trusted confidante to intervene. If the abuse continues after the intervention of others, then it is time to give your relationship an extended vacation, and

I am not implying divorce. I know that leaving an abusive relationship can be challenging and dangerous; therefore, ensure your safety by calling your pastor, bishop, or the police for assistance while you pack your belongings.

Before you leave home, I recommend you have a meeting with your husband. Prepare for it by writing down your thoughts and feelings, and consider having a trusted friend or family member present for support. Calmly and professionally express your disappointment to your husband. Tell him, "When I said yes to marry you, I thought I was saying yes to a mighty, God-fearing man who would love and treat his wife with dignity and respect." Also, let him know that you are at your wit's end, and to keep your sanity and make heaven your final home, you refuse to live under such hostile conditions. Additionally, make it clear that you both need to be apart until he is mature enough to handle marriage as God intended.

Let the face and the smile you wear to church or at home be a true reflection of your emotions. Embrace authenticity, and let your genuine self shine through. I wish you the best as you stroll along your journey.

# Questionnaire

1. What is your reason for wearing a "church face"?

___

2. Have you ever experienced any form of abuse from your husband? Explain.

___

3. Have you ever covered and made excuses for your husband's abusive behavior?

___

4. If you are currently in an abusive relationship, what are you going to do about it?

_____
_____
_____
_____
_____
_____
_____

5. How do you handle disagreement in the home?

_____
_____
_____
_____
_____
_____
_____

6. Who have you reached out to for counseling, advice, or help?

_____
_____
_____
_____
_____
_____
_____

7. Do you continuously pretend as if all is well while you're dying on the inside? If so, explain.

_____
_____
_____
_____
_____
_____

8. On a scale of 1–10, how would you rate your happiness in the home and the church?

_____
_____
_____
_____
_____
_____

9. List a few reasons why you should avoid sharing your story with the church members.

_____
_____
_____
_____
_____
_____

10. If and when you decide to take a break from home and the marital relationship due to repeated abuse, what should you do?

_____
_____
_____
_____
_____
_____
_____

11. Write your prayer pertaining to the subject at hand.

_____
_____
_____
_____
_____
_____
_____
_____
_____
_____
_____
_____
_____
_____
_____

## Avoid Cliques

*Then said he unto the disciples, It is impossible but that offences will come: but woe unto him, through whom they come! It were better for him that a millstone were hanged about his neck, and he cast into the sea, than that he should offend one of these little ones.*
*Luke 17:1-2 KJV*

*A clique is the dwelling place for insignificant people who share the same insecurities.*
*~Damon Johnson*

I overheard someone stated that a clique is "an epidemic that breaks out within the church." Typically associated with schools, colleges, organizations, and workplaces, cliques are exclusive groups of people who are unfriendly to outsiders or newcomers. Like church bullies, never in my wildest dreams did it cross my mind that cliques would be associated with the church. Yet, to my surprise and shock, I discovered that churches are full of cliques.

## Avoid Cliques

Regardless of their reasons for being there, church is a place where everyone should feel welcomed and comfortable, never rejected. Some may be seeking Jesus, while others may be fleeing loneliness and abuse. Some may be in search of love, security, a community, or a sense of belonging. The diversity of reasons for attending church underscores the importance of its inclusivity and community.

In my humble opinion, some people form cliques because they want to feel connected to others. They may long to be a part of a family or community. However, the formation of cliques can lead to division, seclusion, and, tragically, even suicide as the worst outcome. This negative impact on the church community is significant, as it can cause others to stumble or backslide. For example, a clique is an inner circle or group for specific individuals. Individuals outside the circle may feel excluded and inferior and believe they are not good enough to be among some congregants. Hence, it may cause them to leave the church, isolate themselves, and before long, walk away from God. Sadly, cliques can damage the ministry and the body of Christ, therefore, it is our collective responsibility to ensure that everyone feels included and valued in our church community.

Too many times, I have seen women in churches sitting alone in a depressive state because no one speaks to them, eats with them, or befriends them. Perhaps these women do not meet the requirement to be a part of a particular clique. Could it be because they do not drive fancy, top-of-the-line cars or wear the finest suits? Maybe they don't hold a prestigious job or are not highly educated. If you are a first lady or a leader, seek to know and serve those who are excluded from the "elite." Introduce yourself to everyone, especially those who appear to be starving for attention and acceptance. Take them under your wings and groom them. Furthermore, you might teach some of them how to be ladies—how to attire, speak, sit, dine, and much more.

As a church leader, it is your responsibility to engage with new members and make them feel valued and welcomed. Your role is not just to support your husband's ministry, but also to build the self-esteem, confidence, and character of the young members of your church and community. Don't ignore those who need you the most. Try to meet with the new members after the main service at least twice a month. Ask them how they're doing and if they need anything. Let them feel your love and see that you care about their well-being. Remember why you were called and chosen by God. Preach, teach, live, and show them Jesus through your actions and character.

Unfortunately, I have seen many believers backslide and visitors fail to return to church because of the way they were treated, spoken to, and gossiped about. Initially, they felt welcomed and at home, but before long, they were expressing feelings of disappointment, hurt, and rejection. Some left with a terrible taste in their mouth, believing that they overstayed their welcome and all "church people" are alike. They couldn't wait to exit those doors. As born-again believers, we are guilty of wounding hungry souls.

Kingdom woman, I hope you are not easily influenced or swayed. Watch out for those introducing you to their so-called "little group" and inviting you on lunch dates. A few individuals may volunteer to be your tour guide and source of information. Without fear or reservation, they will dictate who you should avoid and to whom you should and should not speak. Pay keen attention to those who always want you to sit with their group and those who may flood you with lavish gifts. Carefully discern

## Avoid Cliques

their motives and intentions. As a significant influencer and leader, lead from the front so you won't be led.

In my opinion, cliques don't have to be viewed as a bad thing if their inner circle is promoting Jesus Christ and treating others as their equal and with love. However, to avoid self-centered cliques in a church, intentionally include everyone in church activities. Back in the day, pastors and those in leadership would visit the homes of new members, visitors to the church, and the sick and shut-ins. Maybe you cannot visit their homes, but you can still reach out to them by telephone. During group meetings or breakout sessions, spend time in each group connecting with different people. Encourage the leaders of each group to be receptive and sensitive to the needs of all attendees without showing favoritism.

# Questionnaire

1. What is your view on cliques in the church?

_____
_____
_____
_____
_____
_____

2. What do you believe is the cause of congregants forming cliques in the church?

_____
_____
_____
_____
_____
_____

3. What is your plan to break up any clique in your church?

_____
_____
_____
_____
_____
_____

4. In your opinion, are cliques a good or bad thing regarding the body of Christ? Explain the destruction caused by cliques in the church.

_____
_____
_____
_____
_____
_____
_____

5. Explain the benefit, if any, of entertaining cliques in the church.

_____
_____
_____
_____
_____
_____
_____

6. How devastating can cliques be to new members, visitors, and new converts?

_____
_____
_____
_____
_____
_____
_____

7. Let's delve into this scenario: How can cliques, if left unchecked, cause division, seclusion, and possibly suicide, among others? How can they damage the ministry and the church and cause others to stumble or backslide?

_____
_____
_____
_____
_____
_____

8. Are you the kind of first lady who supports cliques in the church? If so, why?

_____
_____
_____
_____
_____
_____

9. Explain the ramifications of having cliques in the church.

_____
_____
_____
_____
_____
_____

10. Explain how forming and joining cliques can cause one to miss God, heaven, and their blessings.

_____
_____
_____
_____
_____
_____

11. Write your prayer pertaining to the subject at hand.

_____
_____
_____
_____
_____
_____
_____
_____
_____
_____
_____
_____
_____
_____

## Protect Your Ear Gate

*But blessed are your eyes because they see, and your ears*
*because they hear. For truly I tell you, many prophets*
*and righteous people longed to see what you see but did not see it,*
*and to hear what you hear, but did not hear it.*
*Matthew 13:16-17 NIV*

A gate is an opening for something or someone to enter or exit. Our five senses are known as gates—the eye gate, ear gate, mouth gate, touch gate, and nose gate. The ear gate is a metaphor for the sense of hearing. It is not just a physical organ but a spiritual gateway that allows information and influences to enter our minds and hearts. What you permit to enter through the ear gates can increase or deplete you in more ways than one. It can alter your thought patterns and cloud your judgments.

Have you ever been told by an audiologist not to put anything smaller than your elbow in your ears? Inserting any object into your ears can puncture your eardrum or damage your ear canal. We are also instructed on how to protect our physical ears from noise and water and how to remedy earaches.

However, the spiritual ears are even more sensitive. What you listen to and allow to be absorbed into your spirit may not only affect you physically but will spiritually interfere with your mindset and well-being. Protecting your ear gate means being selective of the conversations you engage in and the speech you allow to enter your life. You have the power to choose what you allow in through your ear gate, which can either lead you to higher and deeper place in Christ or drive you far away from Him. If faith comes by hearing the Word of God, then fear also comes by hearing the words of Satan and his agents. What are you hearing? Is it faith-driven or fear-driven? Avoid listening to negative news that distorts your thinking and can cause chaos within your home, church, and family. Remember, the power is in your hands to protect your ear gate and shape your spiritual journey.

Hearing other people's business can be juicy news to the flesh. The more you hear, the more you want to know. But in the end, how will it positively enhance your spiritual growth? I believe that every church has someone specializing in the news department, and they do not mind volunteering information all year long. Some members will seek to befriend you so they can download all their irrelevant information about church members, neighbors, or the couple around the corner. Such individuals will do anything they can to get the scoop on everyone, including you and your family. They seem to be assigned to destroy churches, relationships, happy homes, and marriages. It's important to remember that their actions can be harmful.

When someone approaches you with information about another person, it is crucial to be an active listener and carefully dissect the content of the conversation. Is it criticism? Is it tale bearing? Is it gossiping or genuine concern for the individual? This discernment is not just important, it is empowering. It is the key to understanding the true nature of the information and its potential impact on your spiritual growth. Will you be encouraged, edified, or terrified by the information shared? Does it line up with your core values and beliefs? Listening to the wrong message can sabotage your faith, stunt your spiritual growth, and prevent you from accomplishing your spiritual assignments. Do not hesitate to shut down anyone who engages in contaminating conversation. Draw a line, put your foot down, and tell them nicely that you are not interested in maligning or assassinating another person's character. If you refuse to close your ears to toxic talk, you will become what you allow your spirit to ingest and digest.

Who you associate with has the power to transform your life, either by leading you to miss your blessings or by gaining favor with both God and man. It is therefore crucial to surround yourself with positive and influential people who will not only challenge you to grow spiritually but also encourage you to become a better person and spur you on to greatness. Keep meditating on the Word of God and seek His heart daily. The environment you create has the potential to significantly impact your spiritual growth and personal development, filling your life with hope and optimism.

## Questionnaire

1. As mentioned in the passage, list your gates.

2. How are you being edified by what you are listening to?

3. Do you think that what you watch regularly helps with your spiritual growth?

4. What are you feeding your spirit man?

_____
_____
_____
_____
_____
_____
_____

5. Can you identify spiritual growth from what you feed your spirit man?

_____
_____
_____
_____
_____
_____
_____

6. What does the Bible say about gossiping or tale bearing?

_____
_____
_____
_____
_____
_____
_____

7. What have you heard that negatively affects your spirit and finds it hard to erase from your mind?

_____
_____
_____
_____
_____
_____

8. What is the danger of not setting boundaries on church members' conversation?

_____
_____
_____
_____
_____
_____

9. How should you act toward anyone who seeks to fill your ears and the atmosphere with negativity, gossip, criticism, and tale bearing?

_____
_____
_____
_____
_____
_____

10. What will be the consequence for refusing to close your ears to toxicity?

___

11. In your own words, what have you gathered from this passage?

___

12. Write your prayer pertaining to the subject at hand.

___

## Never Take Sides

*And the other woman said, Nay; but the living is my son, and the dead is thy son. And this said, No; but the dead is thy son, and the living is my son. Thus they spake before the king. Then said the king, The one saith, This is my son that liveth, and thy son is the dead: and the other saith, Nay; but thy son is the dead, and my son is the living. And the king said, Bring me a sword. And they brought a sword before the king. And the king said, Divide the living child in two, and give half to the one, and half to the other.*
*1 Kings 3:22-25 KJV*

In a given situation, you may instinctively take sides with your friends or loved ones, irrespective of their wrongs. Even when the truth is staring you in the face, you may compromise by seeking ways to justify their actions.

In the church, you may encounter situations in which members are at odds with each other or have an issue with the pastor—who may be your husband. They will try to lodge their complaints secretly, hoping to pull you on their side. Even if the situation involves your best friend or someone you love and respect dearly, it is crucial to remain impartial.

Listen in silence to both parties separately. After listening to each party, call a meeting with both individuals and ask relevant questions. Give your best advice and words of encouragement as you try to solve the problem.

If you can identify who is wrong, let them know how and where they went wrong, irrespective of who may become disgruntled. It's better if the person is upset with you now for speaking the truth and then changes their ways rather than giving them false hope by justifying their action, which can eventually lead to their downfall. *(Open rebuke is better than secret love, Proverbs 27:5)*. This situation requires courage and a commitment to truth, to bring justice and provide solutions. Meanwhile, do not allow anyone to feel misunderstood, guilty, or blamed. If you cannot handle the situation, and it does not involve the pastor, ask him to intervene.

*When a conflict involves the pastor, it's important to seek the help of other church leaders, such as the church mother, deacon, or board members. This ensures the involvement of a higher authority and promotes a sense of community in resolving the issue.*

## Questionnaire

1. What is your plan of intervention for members who are at odds with each other?

_____
_____
_____
_____
_____
_____

2. Have you been tempted to take sides with church members instead of your husband? If so, please explain.

_____
_____
_____
_____
_____
_____

3. How do you plan to keep your members vigilant of the schemes of the enemy?

_____
_____
_____
_____
_____
_____

4. What should you do if a member complains to you about your husband? (If he's the pastor)

___

5. What is your remedy for the mischief makers, gossipers, and talebearers in your church?

___

6. Do you have the guts to tell an individual when he or she is wrong? What is your tactic?

___

7. How would you detach yourself from a discrepancy that involves someone dear to you?

_____
_____
_____
_____
_____
_____

8. What is your understanding of 1 Kings 3:22-25?

_____
_____
_____
_____
_____
_____

9. Have you ever taken sides with someone and regret having done so? If so, what did you learn from that experience?

_____
_____
_____
_____
_____
_____

10. Write your prayer pertaining to the subject at hand.

## Be an Attentive Listener

*My dear brothers and sisters, take note of this: Everyone should be quick to listen, slow to speak and slow to become angry.*
*James 1:19 NIV*

To be an outstanding leader, you must be an excellent listener. Listening is a vital skill along life's journey; it is also an art and a requirement for success. Only through attentive listening can we effectively demonstrate the perfect will of God in our lives. Recap the stories of the prophets and major characters in the Bible. You will see that they all have one thing in common—*listening*. Whether it cost them their throne or their lives, or they became successful as a result, listening was an essential factor. It can be a negative or positive stronghold in one's life; it just depends on *who* or *what* you're listening to.

Just as you are required to be an excellent listener to your husband, you are required to be an excellent listener to your Congregants. Attentive listening is a skill we were not born with but we learn and hone over time. Whenever your members are speaking to you, be attentive and respond with love and a caring attitude. It may not be a complaint or gossip, but rather a genuine concern about the growth of the church. Perhaps they have ideas on how to enhance a department, conduct fundraisers, or improve various ministries. Therefore, instead of shutting them down, dismissing their ideas, or giving them the silent treatment, take a moment to listen without judgment. Do not appear to be in a hurry or too busy to respond.

Moreover, your members may need your opinion or guidance concerning decisions they need to make. They may relate things to you of which you have no interest, but listen to them anyway. Ask God for wisdom, patience, and tolerance. Do not appear uninterested. Allow them to feel as if their problem is your problem, their discomfort is your discomfort, and their pain and concern are your pain and concern. Rely on God's guidance for the perfect response to their situation so that you can provide the right advice or suggestions.

Many people in your church may not have a confidante or anyone trustworthy enough to whom they can pour out their souls. Make it comfortable for your members to approach you respectfully and without fear. Be sympathetic, apologetic, and understanding when needed. Be emotionally and mentally present to those with whom you speak. In the chapter "Be an Excellent Listener," you were enlightened on how to make your husband know that you are listening and engaged in what he is saying. Likewise, during your conversation with your church members, apply the same principles. Reassure them that you are listening by leaning in and making eye contact. You never know what you will learn when you truly listen.

Listening without judgment or restlessness is a sign of expressing love, compassion, and respect toward the individual. Look keenly at the letters in the words *listen* and *silent*. What do you see? Yes, they share the same letters. What's the significance here? Listening requires you to be silent. By being silent, you will hear and learn more.

# Questionnaire

1. How would you rate your listening ability?

_____
_____
_____
_____
_____
_____

2. How do you demonstrate the traits of a good listener?

_____
_____
_____
_____
_____
_____

3. It takes patience to listen attentively. Describe your patience level.

_____
_____
_____
_____
_____
_____
_____
_____

4. Have you ever been told that you do not listen? If so, why?

___

5. How do you plan to perfect your listening ability?

___

6. What have you lost or missed because you refused to listen?

___

7. How do you possess the qualities of an outstanding leader?

___

8. Describe your body language when someone is speaking to you about things that have no interest to you.

___

9. Does busyness get in the way of your listening? If so, how?

___

10. How approachable are you? Is your personality welcoming or intimidating?

_____
_____
_____
_____
_____

11. During your conversation, how should you reassure others that you are listening?

_____
_____
_____
_____
_____

12. Write your prayer pertaining to the subject at hand.

_____
_____
_____
_____
_____
_____
_____
_____
_____

## Delegate

*And Moses' father in law said unto him, The thing that thou doest is not good. Thou wilt surely wear away, both thou, and this people that is with thee: for this thing is too heavy for thee;*
*thou art not able to perform it thyself alone.*
*Exodus 18:17-18 KJV*

Perhaps Moses was known as "Mr. Independent." He tried doing everything by himself and refused to ask for help. One day, Jethro, Moses's father-in-law, looked at him out of concern for his well-being and advised him to seek help or else he will crumble under this great undertaking (Exodus 18: 14-19). The Bible says when Aaron and Hur held Moses's hands up, he was victorious over the Egyptians. Once his hands went down, he was defeated (Exodus 17:10-13).

Along your journey, you will need help; you cannot do it all alone. Do not be afraid to delegate church duties to willing, qualified members. You may feel like a superwoman who can do it all, but I encourage you to learn how to delegate. Share the workload and begin assisting from a manager's standpoint. Identify the roles and departments that need to be filled, and interview individuals who are gifted and excellent at what they do in certain areas. Of course, there are individuals who will cheer you on to do more than you can manage. Be wise as a serpent and harmless as a dove (Matthew 10:16).

Everyone is gifted in a certain area, perhaps multiple areas, and they may be willing to lend their gifts and talents to serve the glory of God. Some are willing to learn what they do not know, and some are efficient but lack speed and confidence. Some may be workaholics and excellent at almost everything. Know the strengths and weaknesses of each willing individual who is driven to serve and delegate according to their experiences, skill set, and willingness.

Distributing the workload among the members may be challenging. You may be tempted to delegate the most important and time-sensitive work to your top performers (workaholics) because they complete assignments in record time—even if it's not their role or department. Think twice before you overload, overwhelm, or burn out your best workers.

Monthly meetings are critical to your departmental workers' growth, unity, and motivation. Consider this an opportunity to revisit your delegation strategy and ensure that everyone knows their assigned department, role, and task. During this period, inquire about possible needs for improvement. Ask how you can better serve them and if the assignments given are being completed accurately. Listen to their input and concerns on various issues. This is the perfect time to address any discrepancies that may exist. Have a one-on-one discussion to identify underlying issues and deal with them before they escalate. As leaders, your role in promoting teamwork is essential. Encourage the members to help each other, especially if someone lacks motivation and is struggling to complete a project. The church succeeds when everyone succeeds.

If you are the first lady, make yourself accessible to the members of every department. Even though you may not be doing the actual tasks, you can supervise or manage in areas where you feel comfortable. Create a team that values excellence and is willing to make a difference in the lives of others, the community, and the body of Christ. Do not wait until the last minute to delegate a task. Tracking the progress of delegated tasks is extremely important. Spend time with those who need encouragement and affirmation.

If a task is not done when expected, never lose your peace or act out of character. There is no reason to yell, be angry, call anyone out of their names, or give the silent treatment. In all walks of life, the unexpected happens. It could be an accident, misunderstanding, delay, or equipment malfunction. Along your journey, learn to be flexible and not overly rigid. When things do not go as planned, read, repeat, and memorize Romans 8:28.

# Questionnaire

1. Why is delegation needed in the church?

   _____
   _____
   _____
   _____
   _____
   _____
   _____

2. Which task would you delegate?

   _____
   _____
   _____
   _____
   _____
   _____
   _____

3. Some leaders are afraid to delegate out of fear, lack of confidence, or the belief that they can do it all. What is your reason for not delegating?

   _____
   _____
   _____
   _____
   _____
   _____

4. What is the deciding factor that makes you choose an individual for a specific task?

_____
_____
_____
_____
_____
_____

5. List some examples of effective delegation.

_____
_____
_____
_____
_____
_____

6. If a task has been delegated, why are you still trying to do it yourself?

_____
_____
_____
_____
_____
_____
_____
_____
_____

7. What is your expectation after delegating tasks?

8. How specific are you when delegating a task?

9. How do you track the growth and unity of departmental workers?

10. What should be your reason for delegating and to whom should you delegate?

11. Do you delegate out of favoritism, professionalism, or experience?

12. Are you overworking those who are dedicated, willing, and hardworking?

13. True or False: I provide support and guidance to those whom I delegate multiple tasks.
_____
_____


14. True or False: If a task is not done when expected, **it is okay** to lose your peace and act out of character.
_____
_____


15. On a scale of 1–10, how would you rate yourself in providing straightforward instruction to individuals to whom you delegate tasks?
_____
_____
_____
_____
_____


16. What are your reasons for missing deadlines?
_____
_____
_____
_____
_____
_____

17. What makes you believe you can do everything without assistance?

_____
_____
_____
_____
_____
_____

18. Do you only delegate tedious tasks and keep the easier tasks for yourself?

_____
_____
_____
_____
_____
_____

19. What protocol do you follow to ensure you are delegating the right task to the right individual, with the right instruction?

_____
_____
_____
_____
_____
_____
_____
_____
_____

20. In your own words, define "delegation."

_____
_____
_____
_____
_____
_____
_____

21. Write out Romans 8:28 three times.

_____
_____
_____
_____
_____
_____
_____
_____
_____
_____
_____
_____
_____
_____
_____
_____
_____
_____

22. Write your prayer pertaining to the subject at hand.

# Intercede

*Pray in the Spirit at all times and on every occasion. Stay alert and be persistent in your prayers for all believers everywhere.*
*Ephesians 6:18 NLT*

A group of women were interceding for a young man who was in jail. While they were praying, they heard a knock on the door. To their astonishment, it was the young man in the flesh, but they didn't believe and thought it was his angel (Acts 12:13-15). That is the manifestation of the power of intercession.

As a kingdom woman, you are called to intercede not only for yourself or family but for nations, countries, continents, families, the church, and other individuals. As you pray, you stand in the gap of those for whom you are interceding. You are a negotiator, constantly imploring to God on their behalf. Along your journey, God will place the names of various people and places in your heart to intercede for them. You have become a spiritual watchman for the souls of God's people. As an intercessor and a watchman, one major duty is to pray intensely (intercede) for your pastor and the church.

An intercessor is one who not only prays, but brings people, places, and things before God as often as possible. Intercessors are **courageous, bold**, and **steadfast**, endowed with heightened **discernment**. They must possess strong **endurance**, be **consistent**, live a **consecrated** life and make **self-sacrifices**. A biblical example is Apostle Paul, who was constantly interceding on behalf of the Ephesians and Colossians (Romans 8:26-27; Colossians 1:9-12; Ephesians 1:15-20). Interceding for others is also beneficial to you as it draws you closer to God. It builds your dedication to prayer, teaches you how to love the unlovable unconditionally, and strengthens your relationship with God. While interceding for others, you are indirectly praying about your own situation, and in the process, you receive deliverance from Satan's deadly grips and the desired healing.

Be prepared to have many sleepless nights and interrupted days, as the burden of the church members and their families, communities, leaders, and children rest heavily in your spirit. When the forces of darkness rise against the church, congregants and other individuals, you may have to stand in the gap. There are battles you will have to fight, strongholds to pull down and destroy, demonic activities to cancel, and sicknesses and diseases to rebuke.

How will you know who to intercede for and when? When a person's name and face, or a particular situation, keeps popping up in your mind, and you can't seem to shake or dismiss it, and that feeling intensifies, it is time to lie prostrate and petition God on their behalf. Perhaps someone's life is in grave danger, or a marriage needs restoration. Possibly, someone is crying out for a financial breakthrough or needs healing of their mind, body, and spirit. You may never know the reason or reasons why individuals are placed heavily on your spirit for you to intercede.

*Intercede*

How many times have you felt the unction to pray for someone, a place, or a particular situation but ignored it? How many times have you heard yourself repeating the name of someone you haven't seen or spoken to in a long time, but paid no attention? How many times have you ignored the urge to pray, only to later hear that something devastating has happened to that person or place? Or suddenly, the person calls and tells you about the turmoil they have been going through. Please, whenever you have the urge to pray for someone or a certain situation, *do not hesitate*. Avoid trying to figure out "why," and do not dismiss the situation as being unimportant. Time is of the essence.

Your spirit man knows what is taking place in the spirit realm. He is *alerting* you to intercept and cancel that demonic assignment before it manifests in the earth realm. Move speedily, block the plans and assignments of the enemy against the individual. Unless the Holy Spirit gives you a specific instruction on what to pray for, cover all areas of that person's life in your prayers.

# Questionnaire

1. Define intercessor and list ten of its attributes.

___

2. How do you feel standing in the gap for those who are experiencing spiritual warfare? What is your most recent experience of seeing your prayers answered?

___

3. What is the difference between an intercessor, prayer warrior, and someone who loves to pray?

___

4. What is your major hindrance when interceding for others?

5. How often should you intercede?

6. For whom should you intercede?

7. What should you do when the Holy Spirit unctions you to pray for someone?

_____
_____
_____
_____
_____
_____

8. What does 1 Timothy 2:1 say?

_____
_____
_____
_____
_____
_____

9. How can you benefit from interceding for others?

_____
_____
_____
_____
_____
_____
_____
_____
_____
_____
_____

10. What is your take away from Colossians 1:9-12, Ephesians 1:15-20, and Romans 8:26-27?

_____
_____
_____
_____
_____
_____
_____
_____

11. How will you know what, when, how, and who to intercede for?

_____
_____
_____
_____
_____
_____
_____

12. Write your prayer pertaining to the subject at hand.

_____
_____
_____
_____
_____
_____
_____
_____

# Chapter 6

# The Church

*Go ye therefore, and teach all nations, baptizing them in the name of the Father, and of the Son, and of the Holy Ghost: teaching them to observe all things whatsoever I have commanded you: and, lo, I am with you always, even unto the end of the world. Amen.*
*Matthew 28:19-20 KJV*

We are the church. However, as it relates to the building where we gather for worship, it is and should continue to be a place of refuge and safety for those who desire Jesus Christ as their Lord and Savior. Everyone who enters through the church doors should be welcomed and feel at home, irrespective of their status, race, accomplishments, or appearance.

Some people see the church as a lifeline and run to it to find hope, a reason to continue living, to find family, someone to love them, and someone with whom they can vent and share their problems. Keep your eyes open for visitors and new converts who may not know anyone in your church but are in need of a friend, a listening ear, or a shoulder on which they can lean and cry. Take a lesson from Jesus' disciples, who were groomed, trained, and taught while in His inner circle. After Jesus' ascension, the disciples did not isolate themselves from the public;

## The Church

neither did they form a "members-only" clique with each other. The disciples gave themselves to the service of God, traveling from city to city, preaching and teaching all nations as they were commissioned to do. In spite of the numerous oppositions and the persecution they faced, they never stopped reaching out to the discouraged and lost souls.

Create a program within the church that is responsible for contributing resources to individuals or groups who are in need, whether in the church or the community. The world calls it "welfare," but you might name it "bless fare." Through this program, members can donate their time to soup kitchens, shelters, or food pantries as well as donate money, clothing, or food. It is vital that people learn about your church and the benefits your church offers. Therefore, ensure that information about your church and its location is publicized. Finding the means and ways to draw people to the church is good, but what would be even better is finding ways to *keep them* once they arrive there. How can you do that?

Humans want to know that they are needed, that they are relevant, and that their services are being utilized. Most importantly, they want to feel a sense of belonging. Establish a rapport with the attendees, individually and collectively. Inquire about their passions, gifts, and talents. Introduce them to the various departments, small groups, programs, or events to which they can apply themselves and feel useful.

The church should not be used to expose or repeat the stories shared with you in private. It is not a social club or a place for politics. At church, individuals are expected to be loved, mentored, encouraged, empowered, and taught the unadulterated Word of God without compromise. May your church be a place that nourishes, grooms, and prepares its congregants to carry out the work of God.

# Questionnaire

1. What is the mission and vision of the church?

_____
_____
_____
_____
_____
_____

2. How relevant is the church today?

_____
_____
_____
_____
_____
_____

3. Do you believe members or visitors are satisfied with your church's programs and services?

_____
_____
_____
_____
_____
_____

## The Church

4. How do you feel after a church service has ended?

_____
_____
_____
_____
_____
_____
_____

5. Would you agree that the present-day church is completely different from the church in the olden days?

_____
_____
_____
_____
_____
_____
_____

6. What are your plans to bring back the mothers of Zion, raise up evangelists, and allow the five-fold ministries to birth in the church?

_____
_____
_____
_____
_____
_____
_____

7. Who or what is considered to be the church, according to the words of Jesus?

_____
_____
_____
_____
_____
_____

8. Why do most people go to church?

_____
_____
_____
_____
_____
_____

9. Some people view the church as a:

_____
_____
_____
_____
_____
_____
_____
_____
_____
_____

10. List five expectations of an individual when they visit your church.

___

11. What do you think about leaders who are lowering the standards of God and compromising His Word to draw young people to the church?

___

12. How do you ensure that members and visitors feel welcome?

___

13. What resources do you have to contribute to the community, charity events, shelters, or rehabs?

_____
_____
_____
_____
_____
_____
_____

14. How will people know about your church?

_____
_____
_____
_____
_____
_____

15. What are your plans to keep members and visitors coming to church?

_____
_____
_____
_____
_____
_____
_____
_____
_____

16. What is your short-term and long-term goal for the ministry?

17. How do you suggest reaching out to the community?

18. What would your "bless fare" program entail?

19. What are your plans to encourage young people to attend church?

___

20. Write your prayer pertaining to the subject at hand.

___

## Teach Your Members How to Treat You

*Walk in wisdom toward them that are without, redeeming the time. Let your speech be always with grace, seasoned with salt, that ye may know how ye ought to answer every man.*
*Colossians 4:5-6 KJV*

It is a sad reality that whenever you get too close or friendly with some people, they tend to overstep their boundaries. They talk down to you as if you are their companion, regardless of where they are or who is around.

How you speak to others and the character you model in the presence of the congregants will automatically reveal who you are. When you show respect and consistently treat members the way you would like to be treated, you are nonverbally teaching others how to treat you. Most will perceive that certain boundaries should not be crossed. Remember, setting boundaries is not a sign of weakness but a powerful tool to maintain healthy relationships. Although in the eyes of many people, you are expected to be perfect, rest assured, everyone may not like or care for you or what you stand for. At the same time, you are expected to be gracious and humble to everyone.

Further, be mindful of your words and the jokes you share. Sometimes, we may jokingly say some things to others, but when those same words are spoken back to us, it doesn't sit well, and we feel offended and sometimes disrespected. An inch is given, and a yard is taken. You do not have to be grumpy, stuck-up, or withdrawn; just be conscious of how you speak and what you allow out of your mouth in the presence of others. Additionally, before the members get too familiar with you, I encourage you to have a members' meeting, with the pastor's permission, of course.

During this meeting, establish some boundaries. State clearly your expectations from each church member and as the body of Christ. Ensure them that you will do your best to meet their expectations as long as they are within reason. Further, you will do everything you can to respect everyone—even the breastfeeding baby—and expect respect in return. This includes listening without interrupting, speaking calmly and respectfully, and refraining from personal attacks. Remember, the purpose of this meeting is to discuss matters that will help you fulfill your mission as a church. Keep this mission in mind as you proceed.

Moreover, it is important to acknowledge that not everyone will agree with you or your decisions, which is normal and acceptable. Everyone is entitled to their opinions and feelings as long as they are expressed with respect. Remind them that the shared goal is to work together for the greater good of building the kingdom of God, and this diversity of thought is a strength, not a weakness.

Throughout the discussion, it is important to maintain a respectful and orderly environment. Tell them that you will not tolerate being yelled at or spoken to in a derogatory manner, especially in the presence of others. You will not accept any hissing of teeth or disturbances while talking. If anyone believes they can overstep their bounds and be met with a smile, they are mistaken. Address any such behavior immediately and directly. Those who fail to adhere to these guidelines may be asked to leave the meeting or face further disciplinary action.

# Questionnaire

1. How will you teach your members to treat you?

_____
_____
_____
_____
_____
_____

2. What is the first thing you should do before getting too familiar with the congregants?

_____
_____
_____
_____
_____
_____

3. What are your expectations of the members and leaders?

_____
_____
_____
_____
_____
_____
_____

4. What should be the agenda of your initial meeting with the congregants?

5. What are the benefits of setting boundaries early?

6. Why is it important to teach others how to treat you?

7. How will you handle those who disrespect you privately or publicly?

8. How do you nonverbally teach others how to treat you?

9. How would you describe the way you have been treated?

10. Write your prayer pertaining to the subject at hand.

## Do Not Let Your Guard Down

*Be sober, be vigilant; because your adversary the devil, as a roaring lion, walketh about, seeking whom he may devour.*
*1 Peter 5:8 KJV*

It is human nature to relax and become complacent after an accomplishment or victory. We become nonchalant as if we have arrived and nothing else matters anymore. We are not as alert or guarded.

Spiritually, when we drop our guard, the enemy moves in to destroy, as he did with Adam and Eve. Kingdom woman, I strongly advise you to never let your physical and spiritual guards down. Being led by the Spirit allows you to discern the enemy's intention from afar. Satan does not care whom he uses deceptively to take you off guard. It is okay to be civil and compassionate to church members without getting too comfortable and friendly. There are individuals who will genuinely need your help. Some may need biblical counseling, while others may need words of affirmation and encouragement. However, be wary of those who are quick to share their personal information with you for no apparent reason. Listen keenly without uttering a word and discern their intention and motive.

When others observe that you are being extra careful and guarded, the more curious they become, wanting to know why. Prying individuals will go to extreme lengths to find out if or what you are hiding. As they patiently wait for you to let your guard down, they are secretly inquiring about your past and present life. If unsuccessful in their inquiries, they may try to sneakily lower your guard by revealing their most intimate or embarrassing personal stories. You may be manipulated into believing you are the only one with whom they share such delicate information. Because they open up and divulge so much to you, you may feel compelled and obligated to share your life's story as well. Without thinking, you go through all the stages of your life, from infancy to adulthood, holding nothing back. There, you've been had.

The moment you let your guard down, you realize you have been broadsided by the person to whom you have confided and regret having shared your personal information. The hearts of men are desperately wicked. Not everyone who seeks to become your friend means you well. Their motives and agendas are influenced by Satan to manipulate and torment you. They were sent to derail and pull you out from under the secret place of God.

Remember that Satan comes as an angel of light; therefore, be vigilant and watch out for his tricks. Protect your heart from pain and protect your feelings from being hurt. Save yourself from disappointment and embarrassment by being observant of and oriented to your surroundings. Avoid being too trusting and chummy with everyone. Do not allow your meekness to be mistaken for weakness.

# Questionnaire

1. What is the first thing that comes to mind after reading this passage?

2. Can you identify with what you have read?

3. What have you learned from this passage?

4. What will you do differently now?

_____
_____
_____
_____
_____
_____
_____

5. Where is your trust level? Do you find it difficult to trust people?

_____
_____
_____
_____
_____
_____
_____

6. In your own words, what does it mean to let your guard down?

_____
_____
_____
_____
_____
_____
_____

7. What are the consequences of letting your guard down?

8. What is your biggest takeaway from this lesson?

9. Moving forward, what will your approach be if you encounter a situation like this?

10. True or False: Satan does not care whom he uses deceptively to take you off guard.

_____
_____

11. Write your prayer pertaining to the subject at hand.

_____
_____
_____
_____
_____
_____
_____
_____
_____
_____
_____
_____
_____
_____
_____
_____
_____
_____
_____
_____
_____
_____

## Express Sincerity to the Members

*My little children, let us not love in word,*
*neither in tongue; but in deed and in truth.*
*1 John 3:18 KJV*

*If* not for the love and grace of God, many of us would prefer to stay clear of individuals who have betrayed, oppressed, deserted and hurt us, wanting nothing more to do with them.

Along your journey, you will encounter individuals who may cause you emotional, spiritual, and perhaps physical pain. Their actions may be the manifestation of the past hurt and pain they have suffered and their consequent vow to trust no one. Their guard is always up as a form of defense, believing everyone is out to hurt them. Some may use weapons of self-centeredness, insubordination, and disrespect as a shield to protect themselves from going through the same trauma all over again. However, if you are a victim of their venom, don't be too hasty to write them off.

Perhaps, if you subdue the spirit of resentment that you feel towards them and open your heart to understand their history and background, you may realize that their behavior was caused by what they have endured.

Deep down, they may be the nicest people you'll ever meet. I am not asking you to ignore their obnoxious behavior but rather to approach them from a place of love and sincerity. Express deep concern about their struggles, pain, well-being, and futures. Allow these individuals to see that you are different from those who have breached their trust. Reassure them that you sincerely want to be there for them, with no strings attached.

As a kingdom woman, you are required by God to remain sincere and trustworthy to everyone while serving whole heartedly even those who lack sincerity, kindness, good wishes, and pure thoughts toward you. Understandably, it is challenging to be nice to those who want nothing but harm for you. Sincerely loving those who continuously inflict emotional, spiritual, and physical pain on you is indeed difficult. Nonetheless, you can overcome hate, resentment, and revenge because greater is He who lives in you than he who influences these foul spirits. With God and time, you will be able to express your authentic inner feelings of love toward individuals who exhibit fakeness and disloyalty toward you. In spite of their ungodly actions, see them through the eyes of God as needing help and deliverance from the claws and influences of Satan.

Perform acts of kindness when needed, with no hidden agenda. Do not be afraid to give compliments for work well done. Acknowledge any efforts made to do better. Sincerity is birth within the heart; you must mean what you say and do. Sincerity includes honesty, so be honest with yourself and maintain the same personality you do when you are around loveable folks. Even those who despise you will respect you for your consistently positive attitude, your approachability, and your authenticity.

# Questionnaire

1. What do you identify with in this passage?

2. Have you ever wanted to stay clear of an individual because of their behavior?

3. Have you read anything in this chapter that alerts you to the danger of missing eternal life with Christ?

4. Can you recall feeling resentment toward anyone? If so, who and why?

___

5. Do you struggle with a judgmental spirit? If so, how do you plan to eliminate it?

___

6. How would you approach someone from a place of love and sincerity?

___

8. How will you express concern for those whose well-being is threatened and who are suffering from emotional pain?

_____
_____
_____
_____
_____
_____

9. Can you be trusted with valuable information and personal secrets?

_____
_____
_____
_____
_____
_____

10. What are the consequences of repeating a matter that you were told not to repeat?

_____
_____
_____
_____
_____
_____
_____
_____

11. Write your prayer pertaining to the subject at hand.

## Do Not Be Quick to Quit

*Know ye not that they which run in a race run all, but one receiveth the prize? So, run, that ye may obtain.*
1Corinthians 9:24 KJV

Are you a quitter or a winner? It has been said that winners never quit, and quitters never win. I am sure you prefer to finish whatever you start and feel successful instead of a failure.

There may be moments when you are brought to tears because you are disrespected, undermined, ignored, and overwhelmed. You may feel like throwing your hands up in the air and saying, "I am done. I have taken enough of this disrespect; I will no longer subject myself to this inhumane treatment." My friend, despite these feelings, please do not give up. Quitting will only make you abort your assignments to empower and bring life, especially to those who have been abandoned and left for dead. Do not miss the opportunity to make a difference in the lives of those who lack confidence and are struggling with low self-esteem. If you quit now, you may never get the chance to help others reach their full potential and find their purpose.

Take a few lessons from Jesus' life while He was on earth. Amid the persecution and humiliation, He did not allow His emotions to get in the way of His mission or assignments. He fulfilled all His assignments. I am sure you know individuals who are going through turmoil, one disappointment after the other, yet they accomplish their goals intentionally. Beloved, irrespective of the discouragement you feel, quitting is not an option. Continue to show up and be the best person you can be to those who need you, and even to those who have caused you pain and discomfort. No matter the circumstances, follow through with what you have started. It is okay to verbalize your disappointments and hurt, but do it without hurting someone else's feelings. Step up to the plate like a fearless soldier and keep on fighting. Quitting has been flushed out of your DNA by the blood of Jesus. Along this leg of the journey, you do not get to quit.

# Questionnaire

1. How likely are you to complete a task you have started?

_____
_____
_____
_____
_____

2. Explain what you were experiencing when you felt like quitting an important task.

_____
_____
_____
_____
_____

3. What are the struggles you faced that made you quit?

_____
_____
_____
_____
_____

4. What could you accomplish if you did not quit?

_____
_____
_____
_____
_____
_____
_____

5. Who would you be today if you did not quit?

_____
_____
_____
_____
_____
_____
_____

6. Do you consider yourself a winner or a quitter? Explain.

_____
_____
_____
_____
_____
_____
_____

7. Define "procrastination."

8. Define "inconsistent."

9. Define "persistence."

10. Define "pursue."

_____
_____
_____
_____
_____
_____
_____

11. Explain how each of the four words above affects your life.

_____
_____
_____
_____
_____
_____
_____

12. What was your reason for wanting to throw your hands up and throw in the towel?

_____
_____
_____
_____
_____
_____
_____

13. Write your prayer pertaining to the subject at hand.

## Do Not Sweat the Small Stuff

*Finally, brethren, whatsoever things are true, whatsoever things are honest, whatsoever things are just, whatsoever things are pure, whatsoever things are lovely, whatsoever things are of good report; if there be any virtue, and if there be any praise, think on these things.*
*Philippians 4:8 KJV*

Wherever people are, problems are inevitable. Therefore, do not take negative whispers to heart, especially if they are not detrimental to your physical self or spirit man. Since you cannot change or control what others say, think, or feel about you, you are not responsible for their actions or reactions. Therefore, do not sweat the small stuff.

Martha was known as "the sister who sweats the small stuff." As a great host and homemaker, she went above and beyond to entertain her visitors. I can just imagine how irritated Martha was with her sister Mary, who sat for hours at Jesus' feet absorbing His every word, while she did all the preparation and serving. It bothered Martha so much that she went to Jesus and said, "Lord, dost thou not care that my sister hath left me to serve alone? bid her therefore that she help me." Jesus responded, "Martha, Martha, thou art careful and troubled about many things: But one thing is needful: and Mary hath chosen that good part, which shall not be taken away from her" (Luke 10:40-42 KJV). In other words, Jesus was saying, "Leave her alone; she is in my presence, and in my presence, there is unlimited joy, peace, and knowledge. You, too, should choose to spend time in my presence."

Physical responsibilities are important and should be carried out, but not to the point where it consumes your entire being, making you too busy to spend time with Jesus. Martha had a choice, and she chose to focus on the physical part. Likewise, Mary had a choice, and she chose to focus on the spiritual aspect of life. Yes, there will be a feeling of discontent when individuals around you reject or make light of their responsibilities. Do not take it personally or "make a mountain out of a molehill," as the saying goes. Perhaps Mary was running on empty and needed to refill her spiritual tank.

If you are in a leadership position or a pastors' wife, do not lose your peace because the church was not cleaned this weekend. Resist the temptation to throw a temper tantrum because the church bulletins were not printed on time or they have one or two errors. Do not become frustrated because the table wasn't professionally set, and someone picked up blue napkins instead of white. Don't worry if your church was not invited to participate at the general convention or conference. There is no need for an anxiety attack because the wrong color of drapes was hung on the pulpit, or the usher did not greet members and visitors in a particular way. All these details are minuscule—the "small stuff." Yielding your emotions to worry and anxiety will only allow the enemy to distract you, drag you off course, and use you to sabotage yourself and the house of God. One gloomy day can turn out to be a lifetime of sadness and misery.

Many people may refuse to participate in the events you organize. Some may criticize the way you structure the departments. Some may believe you are overdoing it, while others may despise you, thinking you are not doing enough. Nonetheless, don't turn the small issues into a gigantic problem. Do not allow yourself to be dismayed over insignificant matters. Nehemiah 8:10 reminds us that the joy of the Lord is our strength. Sweating the trivial stuff will cause you to lose your joy and the importance of your existence and purpose in life. Worrying about small, insignificant things will not erase the stress, trials, or burdens attached to tomorrow; it will only tamper with today's peace and joy. Shift your focus to the important things that really matter. As a reminder to focus on your priorities, please read and memorize Philippians 4:8. Use this scripture to eradicate anything that comes up against your spiritual mind.

As a kingdom woman, I have seen minor issues magnified that turn into mountainous problems that left a devastating effect on families, leaders, and the church. This tendency can be spiritually draining and result in a frustrated life instead of a flourishing one. You will find that letting go of unnecessary burdens or worry will help you not resent those who are not performing up to your expectations, participating in church activities, or assisting with church duties. Sister, breathe! Keep calm during the stressful moments and recognize the tactics of the enemy to keep you in misery and chase people away from you. Worrying is never the solution to any problem. It only magnifies the situation and makes matters worse. Of course, minor difficulties can be irritating, but look at them through a different lens. They serve as a teacher who comes to teach you patience, humility, self-control, and how to stay connected to God. They come to reveal to you that you're focusing on the wrong things and cheating yourself out of true happiness and peace. What the devil intended to use to break you can make you stronger and intentional about changing your mindset and maintaining your peace.

Many individuals who suffer from migraines, high blood pressure, heart palpitations, and anxiety may excessively worry about things that don't matter. Don't lose your nightly sleep and peace of mind over incomplete tasks, whether at home or church. Neither should you allow yourself to be distracted by the immature actions or spoken words of others. If you do, you will be left in emotional turmoil. Remember, the devil comes to steal your joy, kill your peace, and destroy your purpose, potential, and your life. Don't let him. You deserve to be happy as you go along your journey.

# Questionnaire

1. What keeps you up at night?

_____
_____
_____
_____
_____
_____
_____

2. Why are you bothered by the tiny details?

_____
_____
_____
_____
_____
_____
_____

3. How would you explain your peace of mind?

_____
_____
_____
_____
_____
_____
_____

4. Who or what is your mind stayed upon?

_____
_____
_____
_____
_____
_____
_____

5. What would cause church members to avoid you?

_____
_____
_____
_____
_____
_____
_____

6. Looking at your actions and the busyness of your day, what do you spend the most time doing?

_____
_____
_____
_____
_____

7. With whom do you spend the most time?

_____
_____
_____
_____
_____

8. According to your answers to the last two questions, do you believe that God is pleased with you?

_____
_____
_____
_____
_____

9. Write out Philippians 4:8.

_____
_____
_____
_____
_____

10. Write your prayer addressing the subject at hand.

## Choose Your Words Wisely

*Then said he unto the disciples, It is impossible but that offences will come: but woe unto him, through whom they come! It were better for him that a millstone were hanged about his neck, and he cast into the sea, than that he should offend one of these little ones.*
Luke 17:1-2 KJV

As a kingdom woman, and a mighty woman of God, your words should be life-giving and life-changing, not damning or sarcastic. Not everything that comes to your mind or spirit should be uttered, especially if your words will crush the hope or strangle the faith of someone. Resist using words that can damage a person's self-esteem, causing them to feel hurt, embarrassed, belittled, or inferior. Avoid saying words that will ignite a fight.

Some people declare, "I am a plain and outspoken person. I am going to tell it like it is, regardless of whether you like it or not. I am going to speak the truth, whether it upsets or pleases you. I can't keep quiet when I see or hear foolishness. I am someone who calls a spade a spade. Well, that's me."

I have heard these sentiments quite often. They are the words of individuals who lack wisdom, are disobedient to the Word, and lack the love of God. Please take the feelings of others into consideration. Quickly trade places with the individual who you are about to insult. How would you like to receive what you are about to dish out?

I heard a female pastor say to her adult congregation, "You make me sick to my stomach." It is unfortunate that she was unable to control her emotions and anger. Many fights and ill feelings in the church have been caused by the way the pastor, first lady, or lay members handled or did not handle a particular situation, or by the way they spoke to the members. I have heard many individuals complain about how inconsiderate and disrespectful their pastor and their wives are towards them. As they continued to vent, it became clear that some pastors and first ladies do not know how to speak to others. They often come across as self-centered bullies with bossy attitudes, who hurl condescending words toward the members. The disgruntled church attendees stated in response, "Such behavior, we will not tolerate. No tact, no class. We prefer to have someone who will listen, hear, and understand our point of view."

Beloved, avoid responding to everything a person says or wants to do. Be mindful that the individuals whom you are called to lead are not your children. Therefore, if you must respond, filter your words and think before you turn those words loose. Additionally, the pulpit is not the place to address any unsettled matters or dissatisfied feelings you may have about an individual. Take him or her aside and discuss it privately. If the problem cannot be solved in such a manner, call a meeting with the pastor, board members, and the involved person or persons.

*Choose Your Words Wisely*

Negative words can be damaging to the lives of your church members and the community. Your words can break or mend hearts; they can either cause individuals to leave the church or flock to the church. Your words may lead others to resent you or love you. Your words can encourage spiritual and emotional growth or promote stagnancy. What you say and how you say it can determine the mood for the rest of the day or change the course of someone's life forever.

Your words have enormous power. Therefore, erase harmful, corrupt words from your vocabulary. May your words be uplifting, encouraging, and motivating. May they bring healing and deliverance to those who have been afflicted and bound up by destructive words. Take on the character of Christ and free yourself from sarcasm as well. Keeping silent does not mean you are weak; your voice needs to be heard in an encouraging way. Allow your words to be seasoned with grace. Continue to learn how to release positive words into the atmosphere and the lives of others. Words do matter. As you glide along your journey, be transformed by renewing your mind and vocabulary *daily*.

Importantly, do not consider yourself too big to apologize. If you are aware of someone who is hurting because of your words or actions, humble yourself and sincerely apologize. Ask the individual or individuals to forgive you.

*Therefore if thou bring thy gift to the altar, and there rememberest that thy brother hath ought against thee; leave there thy gift before the altar, and go thy way; first be reconciled to thy brother, and then come and offer thy gift* (Matthew 5:23-24 KJV).

*Let no corrupt communication proceed out of your mouth, but that which is good to the use of edifying, that it may minister grace unto the hearers.* Ephesians 4:29 KJV

## Questionnaire

1. Do you have a problem with anger? If so, describe how it can get the best of you and your plan to deal with it.

___

2. How would you describe your actions when you feel frustrated and backed into a corner?

___

3. Are you quick with your words, not caring what comes out? If so, how can you be more mindful of this tendency going forward?

___

4. Identify and list the things that make you upset and frustrated.

_____
_____
_____
_____
_____
_____
_____

5. Can you recall saying hurtful, devastating, or belittling words to anyone? If so, write down their names and apologize so your heart can be free.

_____
_____
_____
_____
_____
_____
_____

6. How do you think God feels when you use your words to hurt others?

_____
_____
_____
_____
_____
_____
_____

7. Are you struggling with using foul, derogatory language? If so, how do you plan to delete that language from your vocabulary?

___

8. What does Proverbs 18:21 say?

___

9. Explain Proverbs 15: 4.

___

10. Elaborate on Matthew 12:36-37

_____
_____
_____
_____
_____
_____

11. How would you feel if someone talked down to you in a crowd?

_____
_____
_____
_____
_____
_____

12. What would your reaction be if your pastor embarrassed you in front of the congregation?

_____
_____
_____
_____
_____
_____
_____
_____
_____

13. Would you consider your members rude and disrespectful if they stopped you immediately when you began speaking to them in a condescending way in the presence of others?

___

14. Have you identified what pushes your anger button?

___

15. What plan do you have in place to ensure that your anger doesn't get the best of you again?

___

16. How could you have handled the disagreement differently?

_____
_____
_____
_____
_____

17. From your heart, sincerely pour out to God your approach to situations in the past and how your words have been damaging. Ask Him to enhance your vocabulary.

_____
_____
_____
_____
_____

18. Write your prayer pertaining to the subject at hand.

_____
_____
_____
_____
_____
_____
_____
_____

## Do Not Settle for Mediocrity

*But ye are a chosen generation, a royal priesthood, an holy nation, a peculiar people; that ye should shew forth the praises of him who hath called you out of darkness into his marvellous light.*
1 Peter 2:9 KJV

My sister, you are exceptional, unique, and a masterpiece. Be the best version of yourself without settling for mediocrity. Allow yourself to shine!

Being the heir of God and joint-heir with Jesus, there is nothing mediocre or ordinary about you. Even though Jesus was not your typical "suit and tie" guy and was always found among the less fortunate, He was never considered ordinary or average.

As a kingdom woman, you are expected to embody and exhibit the spirit of excellence. Your demeanor must be different such that one can identify you as humbly outstanding. Even though you may be criticized, persecuted, and ostracized for your distinguished quality of being, never stoop to the level of the critics. Do not be alarmed if the individuals for whom you went above and beyond shun you or give you the cold shoulder. Success and favor can be irritating to those who struggle with mediocrity and lack confidence. Even those whom you are teaching how to exude the spirit of excellence and become better people may plot your demise. They may create lies to exclude you from social groups or church meetings. The spirit of mediocrity is threatened and intimidated by the spirit of excellence.

Do you remember the story about Daniel? He was thrown in the lion's den by jealous individuals because of his excellent spirit. Nonetheless, it was his spirit that saved him from the hungry lions. Ultimately, the ones who planned his demise and threw him in the lion's den were thrown into the same den, and they and their families were eaten by the same hungry lions. They were plunged into the very pit they dug for Daniel (Daniel 6:1-24).

Irrespective of who may think you are a show-off, or that you are too much, never try to fit in so you can be liked or accepted, because they won't. Being set apart and doing exceptionally well are what your Father desires and expects of you. Therefore, whatever you do, give it your all. Do it to the best of your ability and never let anyone cause you to dim your light or skimp on your assignments.

As a kingdom woman, you are a trendsetter and a visionary. Regardless of the whispers and opposition, take your congregation to the next level, both spiritually and physically—for those who want to be a part of greatness. Strive to leave an indelible mark in the hearts and minds of those with whom you come into contact. Your work and efforts should be so exemplary that they simply cannot be erased or replaced.

*Do Not Settle for Mediocrity*

Being mediocre is beneath you; along your journey as a kingdom woman you are expected to rise above the multiple challenges you face and not settle for mediocrity. Greatness resides in you!

# Questionnaire

1. When you hear the word "mediocrity," what is the first thing that comes to your mind?

___

2. Do you consider yourself mediocre? Elaborate.

___

3. Explain how it makes you feel when individuals with great potential act mediocrely.

___

4. What advice would you give to those who live a mediocre life but have the potential to do much better?

_____
_____
_____
_____
_____
_____
_____

5. Have you ever held back on doing your best because you fear what others may say? If so, explain.

_____
_____
_____
_____
_____
_____
_____

6. Write 1 Peter 2:9 from two different translations other than KJV.

_____
_____
_____
_____
_____
_____
_____

7. How would you describe yourself and the way you conduct business?

_____
_____
_____
_____
_____

8. If you are not living up to your full potential, can you identify why? How do you plan to change that?

_____
_____
_____
_____
_____

9. What are your goals? How many have you accomplished? Is there something you should be doing, but you have drifted off course?

_____
_____
_____
_____
_____
_____
_____

10. Describe yourself physically, emotionally, mentally, and spiritually.

11. Write your prayer pertaining to the subject at hand.

## Avoid Church Bullies

*If anyone wants to be contentious about this, we have no other practice—nor do the churches of God. In the following directives I have no praise for you, for your meetings do more harm than good. In the first place, I hear that when you come together as a church, there are divisions among you, and to some extent I believe it. No doubt there have to be differences among you to show which of you have God's approval.*
*1 Corinthians 11:16-19 NIV*

*I* have heard about bullies in school and on the job, but never in my wildest dreams would I imagine bullies in the *church*.

If your husband is the pastor of a church, depending upon which church body you are affiliated with, he may be transferred to multiple locations over a period of time. Along his journey, he may be asked to preach or pastor in numerous churches in neighboring communities. Disappointingly, the atmosphere in some of these churches may be polluted with the spirit of deception and manipulation. You may also encounter conniving, vindictive, and controlling individuals who must have it their way or no way at all. Those who are being molested by these spirits will seek to manipulate you and coerce you to take sides with them. In other words, you are being bullied into becoming their confederate. If such behavior is present among the congregants, brace yourself for turbulence.

Once there is a slight indication that you are not in agreement with certain behaviors or their way of life, you will be resented and possibly hated. Nothing you do will ever be right in their eyes or supported. You will be perceived as a liability who will interfere with their schemes and possibly expose their follies. Failure to recruit you as their accomplice and puppet may result in a plot against you and your husband to have you dismissed. If it means calling board meetings and forming alliances with the deacons, evangelists, missionaries, or laity to have your husband transferred to another church, they will.

To send you a stern message, church bullies will withhold their tithes, their presence, and their participation in church activities. Some may go out of their way to embarrass you during an ongoing service. With the intention of setting you up, they may inveigle members to get close to you and befriend you. Others may stoop as low as spying on you and your husband's every move to collect evidence in support of their negative claims against you or the pastor. Beloved, along your journey you may encounter some obnoxious church folks. Be observant and aware of your surroundings.

Do not succumb to the pressure of *church bullies*.

1. In your own words, define "church bullies."
___
___
___
___
___
___
___

2. From your definition, can you identify anyone in your church with those traits? How does it make you feel?
___
___
___
___
___
___
___

3. What is your strategy to deal with church bullies?
___
___
___
___
___
___
___
___
___

4. What would your reaction be if someone tried to manipulate you into taking part in illegal, immoral activities in the church?

_____
_____
_____
_____
_____
_____
_____

5. Are you a person who tries to please everyone and wants everyone to love you? If yes, explain why and how you plan to change this tendency.

_____
_____
_____
_____
_____
_____
_____

6. If you know for sure that a member is plotting your demise or downfall, what would be your course of action?

_____
_____
_____
_____
_____

7. How sensitive are you to fake friendships? Is there a trigger or some form of alert? Explain.

8. What will you do about those who are bullying and manipulating other members in your church?

9. Have you ever been approached or bullied in church? How did you handle it?

10. Write your prayer for church bullies—not only in your church, but in churches worldwide.

## Ministries/Departments

$\mathcal{W}$ithin most churches, there are many ministries and departments, to which members are assigned as volunteers or paid workers. Listed below are a few that may already be in your church; if not, you can implement them.

| | |
|---|---|
| Bless Fare | Event Planning/Décor |
| Communication/Media | Fundraising |
| Prayer Team | Maintenance |
| Usher Board | Financial |
| Sunday School | Mission |
| Children's Ministry | Choir |
| Music | Evangelism |
| Administration | New Convert/Visitor |
| Altar workers | Welfare |
| Hospitality | Bible Study |

Seek God's direction and write your prayer for the right ministry department for you.

---| Final Thoughts |---

## From My Heart to Yours

*Kingdom Women—women who are deeply committed to their faith and actively involved in their church community*

Look closely at the graphic design on the front cover of this book. It depicts a woman embarking on a tedious journey alone, carrying her baggage and trying to balance herself on a thin line. This image symbolizes the many roles and responsibilities that women often juggle, and the loneliness that can accompany these tasks. She is multitasking and will do whatever it takes to complete her work and reach her destination. Her determination mirrors the reality of life.

Despite all you do, perhaps you, too, feel unappreciated and alone in carrying out your duties. Although women, particularly Kingdom Women, are rarely recognized as the driving force or influence behind their husbands' success, like closing significant deals and scaling major companies, everyone looks to women to single-handedly get tedious jobs done. From husbands to congregants, family members to friends, and even coworkers, everyone assumes women have the skill set to accomplish any assignment.

## Final Thoughts: From My Heart to Yours

Because marriage is a part of Kingdom Women's journey, you anticipated being married would put an end to you spending time alone. Instead, it came as a shock when you found out that you're married but still lonely. Now you are left with many questions: "Who am I? Why do I feel ignored and deserted? Why am I married and lonely?"

Dear reader, you may have given your all to the children, family, ministry, church, and others, but never remained still long enough to engage in self-care. This is your time to put the oxygen mask on your face first.

The essential takeaway from this message is not so much about being married and lonely, but what transpires along **the journey**. It's for you to have first-hand knowledge of the various paths you may take, the many hats you may wear, the departments in which you may serve, and the major duties you assume along your journey as a Kingdom Woman. In addition to highlighting marriage, relationships, love, and intimacy, this guide brings awareness to the other areas in which you may engage as you travel along life's pathway. Also, it exposes the fact that despite your role, you may experience extreme loneliness, even when surrounded by many people.

Recently, I hosted a surprise 60th birthday celebration for one of my five sisters. The following day was an ordinary one. The birthday girl went to work while everyone else—her siblings, cousins, nieces, and nephews—stayed home. I decided to continue the celebration and booked a stretch limousine for all of us to go to lunch at a fine waterfront restaurant in Cape Canaveral, the port for the cruise lines, a 45-minute drive away. It was a spontaneous act of self-care and a celebration of life—a reminder that we don't need a special occasion to treat ourselves and others.

Beloved, be intentional about providing genuine self-care. Don't wait for special occasions to celebrate you. Do this regularly, not just on birthdays or anniversaries. Now is not the time to tune out, get weary, host pity parties, or give up on your dreams, desires, or potential. Be inspired , I encourage you to celebrate yourself every day in your own unique way. You don't need an excuse to do so; your existence is enough.

Although you are here to assist others on their journeys, it is crucial to engage in self-care practices to take care of others effectively. I applaud you for all your efforts to ensure that you do your job outstandingly well. But remember, you are significant, and it is an absolute necessity to take care of yourself in this process. Self-care requires much more than doing your nails, getting a facial, or spending a day at the spa. My sister, be deliberate about delegating various tasks so that you can sleep better and be less fettered by your many responsibilities. Eat three balanced meals regularly without rushing; visit the doctor for your annual checkup; and get adequate rest and exercise.

Kingdom woman, regardless of who refuses to appreciate you or spend time with you, be intentional about valuing your own existence. Be deliberate about loving and spending uninterrupted time with yourself. For all you do for others, you deserve to be rewarded. Pamper and celebrate yourself without feeling guilty. I love you, sister.

When like-minded individuals come together, their unity exudes strength and power. My friend, I encourage you to join forces with your husband and do mighty exploits for God. Couples can create an excellent marriage by prioritizing each other's needs and spending quality time together. Remember, God should always be at the center of your marriage, providing a strong foundation and guide for your relationship.

*Final Thoughts: From My Heart to Yours*

Whether you're married or single, you have the power to shape your future. I pray that loneliness will no longer be your portion. I encourage you to foster a strong, enduring relationship with God and continuously activate your faith. This unity with God is a powerful tool that can transform your life and relationships.

*Married and Lonely: Along the Journey of Kingdom Women* is a tool to empower, encourage, and transform the lives of those struggling with loneliness. Go! Share what you discovered and use it to empower and encourage others.

*…For unto whomsoever much is given, of him shall be much required: and to whom men have committed much, of him they will ask the more.*
—Luke 12:18


Sincerely

*Evangelist Jasmine Gordon*


*Disclaimer: As previously mentioned, I am not a pastor's wife and never have been. However, as a Transformational Life Coach and one Kingdom Woman to another, I have encountered and overcome many of the challenges and feelings of loneliness that I discuss in this study guide. This guide is meant to encourage, enlighten, and uplift you as you navigate life's pathway.*

# Closing Prayer

*Lord, your Word said whom you love, you chasten. In each chapter of this book, I experienced your love, felt the rebuke, acknowledged the confirmations and received the corrections. Father, I have seen where I went wrong in many instances, and I repent for being disobedient to your Word. Forgive me, O God, for entertaining the spirit of rebellion. Heavenly Father, I admit that I have walked out of your perfect will. I have done and said things I shouldn't have. Please forgive me.*

*Lord, I thank you for this book. Indeed, you are an on-time God. You showed up when I needed you most. Father, I must confess that this book has become my mirror. It reflects and reveals my flaws, weaknesses, and strengths. It motivates me to search, critique, and assess my actions and behavior. As a result, I am a better person today. O Sovereign God, I rededicate my heart, mind, soul, and spirit to you. Continue to work on me, O God, and draw me closer to you each day so that I can experience your power, glory, and anointing.*

*Abba Father, help me to love others the way you love me as I walk in my victory. In Jesus' name, I pray. Amen.*

## Interactive Questions for You and Your Spouse

*H*ere are some questions and tips to keep the communication ongoing throughout your marriage. These questions will provide feedback from your spouse on the marriage, your relationship with each other, and his thoughts and disappointments. When asked at the right time, they should give you great insight into his innermost thoughts. Avoid asking all of these questions at once. Choose an irresistible one that will spark an interesting conversation and then take it from there.

1. How was your day? How successful was it? I assume you have gotten most, if not everything done.

2. By the way, how is your family doing? You know I do not mind any member of your family spending a weekend with us.

3. How can I help you execute your plans and bring them into fruition?

4. Where do you see us five years from now?

5. When did you know that you loved me and wanted us to spend the rest of our lives together?

6. What is your vision for your ministry, and how can I be of assistance?

7. Have you had any revelations lately? What is God saying to us as the church?

8. Honey, how can we rebuild the altar of God in our home again?

9. What do we need to put in place to ensure the growth of our prayer and fasting life?

10. Have you ever thought about hosting a crusade or a revival? That's a great way to win souls for the kingdom.

11. Someday in the near future, we could plan a mission trip to some third-world countries. What do you think?

12. Lately, the youth/young people have laid heavily on my heart. What can we do to reach them? Any suggestions?

13. Honey, have you noticed that COVID has left a lot of marriages and churches in disarray, but we are still standing strong? What is so special about us?

14. What is the one thing you would like to change about our relationship and why?

15. Is there anything I can do to make you happier and more comfortable?

16. Do you think we have a trust issue? If yes, how can we build trust for each other?

17. Have I ever disappointed you? In what way? How can I fix it?

18. Do you believe we have given all of ourselves to each other?

19. What do you expect from me as a wife?

20. How satisfied are you with me as a person and as your wife?

21. How am I doing in the respect department? Have I shown you adequate respect?

22. What would you like me to work on to enhance our marriage and relationship?

23. Honey, let's talk about children. How many would you like and how far apart? Do you have any names in mind?

24. When should we start having children?

25. How is my overall performance with our finances, children, church, home, and you?

26. How can I help you carry the load of the ministry?

27. What would you like us to do regarding disciplining the children?

28. We've been renting for a long time. How can we pool our resources together and purchase our own home?

29. How can we make each other feel more secure?

30. I know nothing is guaranteed, but how can we prove that we will be there for each other, no matter what?

31. Honey, if you are in a bad mood and do not want to be bothered, what do you expect of me, so I won't keep pressing to find out what's wrong with you?

32. How do I show you that your ideas, opinions, dreams, and visions are just as valuable to me as they are to you?

33. How do you feel about us—the marriage, ministry, and our relationship?

34. How can you assure me that you hear and understand my concerns and what's in my heart?

35. What are your long-term plans for us as a family?

36. What can I do to ensure that you will be there with us and for us during times of disaster?

37. If you should decide to pursue another career, what would you like me to do to help you fulfill that dream?

38. What would you do to support me should I decide to pursue my goals?

39. As your wife, what accomplishment in my life would bring you great joy?

40. Together as husband and wife, and as a great team, what would you like us to achieve together?

41. What would be your first reaction if you see me drifting away from Christ?

42. If you could change anything about me, our marriage, ministry, and relationship, what would it be?

43. What do you love about our marriage?

44. How satisfied are you with our sex life?

45. In what areas do we need improvement, if any?

46. Who do you believe is better with budgeting and handling our finances? Who should handle the finances?

*Interactive Questions for You and Your Spouse*

47. As your wife, do I make you feel like a man? Do you feel respected, honored, and loved? If not, how can I make it up to you and be a better wife and lover?

48. I have a bucket list, do you? What are some of the things on your list that you would like to do before you die?

49. How will I know when to give you a break to collect your thoughts versus giving you a hug and lying in your arms silently?

50. How will I know when to encourage and uplift your spirit or leave you alone without saying a word?

(Tip): Don't forget to express your emotions. "Hey hon, I just want to tell you that I love and appreciate you for being a supportive and understanding husband." "Babe, thanks for being my source of strength and a dedicated father to our children."

# About the Author

Evangelist Jasmine Gordon, born Nichole Gordon, is on a mission to win souls for the Kingdom of God. Much like "John the Baptist," she is the voice crying out NOT in the wilderness but over the airways and into the atmosphere, encouraging individuals to repent, turn away from their sinful lifestyles, and foster their relationship with God.

Jasmine was born on the island of Jamaica to a large family: three brothers and five sisters. Raised in a Christian home, she grew up imbued with the love and fear of the Lord, so it was only fitting that she embarked on a steadfast spiritual journey, which eventually led her to add "author" to her growing list of credentials.

Jasmine pursued her education in evangelism at the Manhattan Bible Institute in New York and has traveled as an international evangelist. She has authored six published books and is a radio and television personality and a gospel recording artist of three gospel CDs. In 2005, on the Gil Bailey Gospel radio show, she earned the coveted award of "Best Original Song of the Year" for her song, "I'm on Fire." As an intercessor, she went on to record two CDs on prayer, as instructed by God.

Jasmine's gifts and talents span many fields. She is a chaplain and the founder of Ministries Without Boundaries Int'l, a nonprofit organization in which she serves the needs of single parents, the less fortunate, and the underprivileged. Since Mother's Day 2011, Jasmine has put a smile on the faces of many individuals in and around her community of Palm Bay, Florida, by hosting an annual free banquet and concert. She strongly believes that if people's earthly needs are met, they will be inclined to hear her message of hope.

Despite her numerous titles and accomplishments, Evangelist Jasmine prefers to be called "servant." She began writing her first manuscript in 2003 but did not publish her first book until 10 years later. Since then, she has written multiple books and published six. Jasmine, a **communicator**, believes that she has been called to be a mouthpiece for God in preparing the bride for the bridegroom. Hence, she speaks clearly and loudly through her books, gospel CDs, television, and radio, which she considers to be her evangelist tools.

*As a chaplain and a highly sought-after mistress of ceremonies(MC), Jasmine is available to conduct weddings, graduations, anniversaries, concerts, and birthday parties. She is also a transformational life coach, business and relationship consultant, and motivational speaker for seminars, workshops, conferences, revivals, crusades, and prayer breakfasts.*

With this busy schedule, Jasmine still finds time to be a wife and a mother to her 37 years old son and two grandsons and to do what she considers her secular ministry: a professional nurse and administrator and owner of an assisted living facility. This is a testament to her commitment and selflessness in continuously serving others.

Those who know her and have been touched by her presence and ministries believe that she may well be the next legendary philanthropist in her community. She is constantly seeking ways to inspire and uplift people. Indeed, she is a woman on fire for God and devoted to His guidance and commandments. The future holds many possibilities for evangelist, chaplain, mentor, author, and coach Jasmine. Her audience eagerly anticipates what will come next in her many offerings.

**Other Books by Jasmine Gordon**

*Fear Not! There is Still Power in Prayer*

*38 Reasons for Unanswered Prayers*

*Daily Restorational "52 weeks of Devotion"*

*Prayer Made Easy: "Is it a Challenge for you to Pray?" Vol.1*

*"Secret Struggles: Things We Don't Talk About" Liberty Journal*

*Married and Lonely: Along the Journey of Kingdom Women*

**Books Coming soon:**

*The Power of 30 Second Prayers*

*Word Search Puzzle Book*

*10 Benefits of Forgiveness*

## Contact Information:

Mwb8870@gmail.com
718-781-0671 or 804-720-6080

**Miss Gordon is available for speaking engagements:**

- Seminars
- Workshops
- Conferences
- Revivals
- Crusades
- Prayer Breakfasts
- Coaching
- Consultant

**She is also available as a chaplain and a highly sought after emcee for:**

- Weddings
- Graduations
- Anniversaries
- Concerts
- Birthday Parties

**Be sure to book Jasmine for your next event.**

www.ingramcontent.com/pod-product-compliance
Lightning Source LLC
Chambersburg PA
CBHW080419230426
43662CB00015B/2144